Expert @ Excel: For Beginners

And

Expert @ Excel Pivot Tables

Table Of Contents

Expert @ Excel: For Beginners

Expert @ Excel Pivot Tables

Expert @ Excel:

For Beginners

A Step by Step Guide to Learn and Master Excel to Get Ahead @ Work, Business, and Personal Finance

By reading this document, the reader agrees that under no circumstances is the author responsible for any losses, direct or indirect, which are incurred as a result of the use of information contained within this document, including, but not limited to, — errors, omissions, or inaccuracies.

Introduction

Whether you're a business owner looking for a new way to make operations a little more seamless, a housewife trying to keep the family finances in proper order, or even a college professor struggling to keep all of those grades and lesson plans in check, there's a lot to gain out of learning the ropes of Microsoft Excel.

First released in 1985 for Macintosh and 1987 for Windows, Microsoft Excel is a software that provides users tools to organize and calculate data using a spreadsheet system. The software is one of the standard inclusions of the MS Office Suite, and is used across different professions and contexts to make a variety of operations seamless, easy, and orderly.

Unfortunately, however, lots of people don't fully understand just how helpful MS Excel can be. If you're one of the many who isn't completely aware of *how* to use the platform, you probably only opened it once or twice to make a standard table... and nothing more.

While it is true that the MS Excel software is potentially the greatest bedrock for making tables and charts of a wide variety, there is *so much more* that it can do. From easing computations, to organizing data, to teaching the basics of *programming* - yes, the mastery of MS Excel might just be the next qualification you can proudly display on that updated resume.

Now you know the promise of Excel, the question is - how can you learn it? No doubt, opening up that software and trying to learn the ropes without a reliable guide can be pretty perplexing. Even with basic definitions for the different operations and controls available, it's hard to fully comprehend how to use them. So, what's a beginner to do?

Don't worry - we've got you covered. In this definitive guide, we're dishing out everything you need to know about how to use excel, including some of the more technical mumbo jumbo that might be difficult to figure out by yourself. This easy, step-by-step guide was designed to divide the MS Excel software into simple, clear, and concise chunks of information that you can effortlessly digest so you can make the most of the program without a fuss.

So, are you ready to become an Expert @ Excel? Let's get started.

Chapter 1 - The Fundamental Importance of MS Excel Knowledge

Did you know that up to 78% of middle-skill jobs (those that require employees to have at least a high school diploma) require applicants to be proficient in MS Excel? A study conducted by the Wall Street Journal found that those who were able to prove their mastery of the program were set to receive up to 30% more than their peers in terms of compensation.

True enough, companies are starting to value this type of skill more and more because it offers one basic benefit for employers - more efficient work completion.

Excel gives workers the opportunity to organize data, project future numbers, and do it all with little error, thanks to the software's intelligent list of available formulas. So, employers stand to have much more accurate representations of their metrics - both present and projected - if they have workers who are masters at Excel.

But there's far more to Excel than just being a potent addition to your resume (although that in itself should make it obvious why you need to add it to your list of skills.) Consider the benefits it offers:

Narrow Margin for Error

Perhaps what makes MS Excel far more ideal than any other software in the same niche is the fact that it's not prone to error. Numbers need to be accurate, regardless of whether you're crunching them for your company or keeping them on record to track your household's expenses. The slightest mistakes could cause you to spend more or save less, which can take a toll on your overall financial situation.

The beauty of MS Excel is that it's incredibly *visual*. Numbers that are linked together by way of formulas and 'IF' statements change in real time when one facet of the relationship is manipulated. So, you can see direct outcomes between numbers and how they affect each other by moving values around.

Working with numbers can be tricky, and sometimes, it's hard to see where we might have gone wrong with our computations. Fortunately, software like MS Excel make it possible to organize data and crunch numbers with a very narrow margin for error. This doesn't only save you time, but also spares you from the possibility of miscalculating crucial information.

Efficient Workflow

Efficiency is something we all want - whether we're working on a report for our boss or simply trying to finish filing our taxes. After all, time is money. Unfortunately, however, working with data can take up a *whole lot* of time. In a lot of ways, this ties in with the fact that in general, computations can be prone to error.

In our effort to make sure we've got all the data laid down straight, we might take a little extra time just to go over information and make sure nothing's amiss. But because we can't all have the luxury of time, programs that make the process of working with numbers faster can be highly favorable.

Employers typically prefer employees who can work with MS Excel because it saves a lot of time. The software itself is user-friendly and easy to use, so data management can be made much less time-consuming than traditional methods. In essence, all you really need to do is punch in the numbers and apply the necessary formulas, and that's it.

Increases Employee Value

As was mentioned earlier, mastery of MS Excel can significantly increase the value of an employee. So much so, that they can be given significantly steeper salaries than their counterparts who aren't expert at using it.

This is simply because it gives them an edge that employers can utilize later on. In knowing how to use the software, these individuals can be delegated more tasks and can be relied upon to deliver accurate results.

If you're looking for a way to make your resume look more appealing to the HR department, it's highly recommended that you nerd it up and learn MS Excel. This won't only increase the chance of a hire, but also potentially bump up your initial salary.

Versatile and Flexible

There's a lot to love about Excel, so it's really not just for workers and businessmen. The versatile program offers an array of functions that can be handy in a lot of different contexts. For instance, it also works as a wonderful tool for household expenses, personal finance, and forecasting.

The fact that it was designed to be user-friendly essentially indicates that it was made for anyone and everyone. So, don't think that just because you're not looking to land a job that you won't have a reason to use Excel.

Aside from dealing with numbers, Excel spreadsheets are also particularly handy when organizing written information. Lesson plans, schedules, travel itineraries among others can be made far easier to comprehend and access using the spreadsheet system, thanks to its highly visual characteristics.

But there's far more to the software than what you'll learn at the beginner level. In many cases, Excel has been used time and again as an introduction to programming. Featuring a close connection with the logic of programming, there is no other MS Office software that offers the potential for coding that MS Excel does. The software even leverages Visual Basic - a programming environment that lets you adapt your Excel spreadsheet to reflect the functions and operations that you specifically need. For those who are well versed in this obsolete yet extensive programming language, MS Excel can be used for almost every function imaginable, making it a heavily versatile program like no other.

Who Needs MS Excel?

Assuming that the use of Excel is strictly limited to professionals and employees discredits the software's inherent multifaceted nature. There are lots of different people who might be able to benefit from Excel - from the pros all the way down to housewives. Seeing its beauty simply depends on how well you understand just what it can do.

Business Owners

If you own a small start-up business, then you might not have the funds to spend on expensive business management tools and software. But there might just be a suitable alternative sitting on your desktop. MS Excel makes a great foundation for creating dynamic reports that reflect your business performance.

Charts can showcase progress, growth, and sales, formulas can make it easy to see your ROI, and the spreadsheet format just makes it simpler to keep all of your data in a neat and organized manner. This quick and easy platform essentially makes bookkeeping a breeze, saving you both time and money without sacrificing the accuracy of your records.

Aside from that, Excel is also commonly used to

present projections. Hopefuls who want to own a business typically leverage excel to show lenders the anticipated cash flow of a proposed business. This helps create a clear picture of how a venture is expected to perform, and assures financing entities that the money they lend can and will be paid off over the course of operations.

If you've got a small workforce that's still a little too big for you to be able to handle with the good ol' pen and paper combination, then you can use Excel as a rudimentary employee management system. You can fashion a spreadsheet to contain information on each worker, and keep tabs on whether their benefits have been paid for and how much they've been getting paid.

Company Employees

As mentioned earlier in this chapter, Excel mastery can significantly improve an employee's value as well as make their work more efficient and organized. Workers who are well-versed with MS Excel can leverage their skills to work with numbers more accurately over a shorter period of time. This can be exceptionally beneficial especially if you've delegated the task of working with numerical data.

Some employers even go as far as tasking their

workers to generate reports to be presented to the board of directors. If you're but a humble worker ant in the intricate workforce, then you might think that task to be herculean. Fortunately though, with software like Excel, you can create polished and professional reports with little fuss.

Private Individuals

How have you been keeping tabs on your personal and household expenses and finances? No doubt, you might have noticed how your spending can go a little overboard at times, and how your savings might not actually look the way you want them to. Experts say that this discrepancy between your expectations and your financial reality can be attributed to poor record keeping.

Getting a firm grip on your finances can help you reach your personal goals at the right time. For instance, if you aim to purchase your first house after 5 years of renting, you might have to save a specific amount every month in order to turn that objective into a reality.

Unfortunately, if you can't really *see* where all your money is actually going, you might find yourself scratching your noggin at the end of each month, wondering where things went wrong. This is when you might want to use a more orderly and organized representation of your cashflow so you can call the right shots before you make another purchase.

Excel's visual spreadsheet format makes it incredibly easy to get a clear picture of your cashflow. Sorting data is straightforward, allowing users to sort their numbers by fashioning customized tables so that information can be organized under their designated categories.

	A	B	C	D	E
		MONTHLY EXPENSES			
1					
2		CASH-IN	CASH-OUT	RUNNING BALANCE	
3	SALARY	4,500		4500	
4	FOOD		550	3950	
5	GAS		400	3550	
6	KIDS' ALLOWANCE		700	2850	
7	RENT		980	1870	
8	UTILITIES		800	1070	
9	SAVINGS			1070	
10					

Educators

On average, teachers and college professors handle about 60 students per grading period. That means 60 unique collections of grades, reports, assignments, and other markers for academic performance. On top of that, educators also have to organize and handle a variety of learning topics, all of which need to be delivered on unique schedules, depending on how far along a specific class is in relation to the syllabus.

While old school methods of record keeping are still utilized widely in the academe, digital trends have taken over most schools with administrative bodies encouraging teachers to use their computers for grades more often in order to improve efficiency and accuracy, and as well as limit the amount of paper consumed by these institutions.

For educators, spreadsheets can be used to divide logs by section. This makes it easier to see what lectures have been delivered to specific classes to keep track of the course outline they've covered. This also helps with scheduling, so that teachers can anticipate what lectures need to be delivered next.

Because the grades a student receives over a period are computed and often averaged at the end of each grading period, it helps to have them all in one organized sheet. Once all the numbers have been accurately collected and logged, educators can simply apply the necessary formula to come up with the student's final grade. This eliminates the need to compute each grade manually which doesn't only eat time, but also entails the risk of inaccuracy.

Needless to say, MS Excel can be an indispensable tool in a variety of contexts, so learning the ropes and becoming an expert at MS Excel can be a smart strategy to streamline all the different tasks you do whether at home or at work.

Now that you see just how versatile the software can be, it's time to dive right in and learn the basics to help you achieve Excel expert status.

Chapter 2 - Face to Face with the Excel Interface

The first step towards mastering MS Excel is familiarizing yourself with how it looks. If you've only ever used the software once or twice before, you might feel overwhelmed whenever you see all of those buttons, tabs, and toolbars. No doubt, this particular MS Office program has the most commands compared to most others, and even provides users the opportunity to learn the basics of programming - which you'll learn more about later on.

But for now, it's important that you get the hang of the basic MS Excel interface, so you can confidently navigate the software and its extensive list of commands and functions.

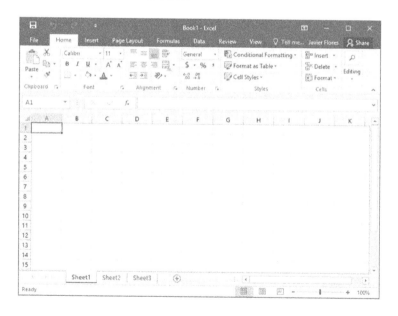

The Basic Elements

Looks like quite a doozy, doesn't it? While it might seem like absolute madness right now, all of those functions and buttons will make complete sense with a little review. First up – you need to understand what all of the different software's interface elements are for.

Quick Access Toolbar

At the topmost area of the screen (upper right-hand side), next to the file title, you'll find the *quick access toolbar*. This is where you can designate commands that you frequently use. In the given example, the user allotted a space for the save, undo, and redo functions. Clicking on the downward pointing arrow next to the quick access icons gives the user the option to add other commands.

Ribbon Tabs

Along the upper half of the screen, just below the file name and quick access toolbar are the ribbon tabs. These tabs allow users to shift the display to feature various options categorized based on their functions. For instance, under the *Home* ribbon tab, you'll find the basic features related to formatting the data you've entered.

Under the *Insert* ribbon tab, users will find options related to adding elements to their spreadsheet such as data from other existing files, images, shapes, and charts, among others.

Ribbon

The *ribbon* is the horizontal section of features that changes as you select different ribbon tabs. Here, you'll find all of the different options and functions you can choose to edit, arrange, and customize your data and your file. Under each ribbon, options are further subdivided into sections. In the example above, you'll see that under the *Home* ribbon tab, the ribbon features including *clipboard, font, alignment,* and *styles,* to name a few.

Formula Bar

The formula bar is the section of the interface where you can see the input of the selected cell. The information in the formula bar changes depending on the cell that's currently active.

If the contents of the cell are purely typed data like raw numbers or characters, then the information reflected in the formula bar will be exactly the same. However, if the data displayed in the active cell is the result of a formula, the information in the formula bar will showcase the formula used to arrive at that specific value.

A1			Q fx	500
	A	B	C	D
1	500	500		
2	349			

In this example, cell A1 contains the actual value '500', so the formula bar reflects the same information.

B1			Q fx	=A1-A2
	A	B	C	D
1	500	151		
2	349			
3				

Upon clicking cell B1, you'll see that the value '151' is not raw input. Instead, it was arrived at by subtracting the contents of A2 from the data in A1. This can be observed by checking the information indicated in the formula bar, which in this case, displays the formula '=A1-A2'.

Cell Reference Number

The cell reference number can be found towards the left of the formula bar, indicated inside the *Name Box*. In this small section, you'll see which cell is

25

currently selected. Users also have the option to type the specific cell destination they want to select if it's too far out of view.

Column and Row Headers

The cells are given reference numbers based on where they lie relative to the column and row headers. As the columns and rows intersect, cells are formed. The column designation is represented by a letter, and the rows are represented by numbers. Thus, cell reference numbers are composed of letter and number combinations.

The entire worksheet space is composed of a number of cells. In the most recent MS Excel versions, there are a total of 17,179,869,184 cells in each spreadsheet.

Spreadsheets

Each Excel file is composed of spreadsheets. Think of these as pages for your file, allowing you to create and organize data into separated categories. At the bottom of the screen, you'll see a small tab labeled 'sheet 1'. As you add more sheets, the software will generate more tabs to allow you to switch between each sheet.

On top of that, users also have the option to rename each sheet. In this example, the user chose to designate each sheet to a specific year to prevent data from one period from mixing in with another. This makes a great solution especially for business owners who want to generate accurate projections and records for each fiscal year.

Status Bar

At the very bottom of the screen, you'll find the status bar. This section gives users an idea as to the current worksheet and keyboard conditions. For instance, users have the option to customize the status bar so that it shows whether the caps lock, num lock, or scroll lock features are currently activated.

An In-Depth Discussion of the Ribbons

Now that you're familiar with all the parts of MS Excel at a glance, it's time to get a little more technical and dive into the intricacies of the most magical element of the program - the ribbons. This collection of features is where you'll find all of the different commands and customization options available to help you format your data the way you want it.

The Home Ribbon

The first ribbon and the one set as the default ribbon that shows as soon as the user opens the software is the *Home Ribbon*. This features the basic options and commands that are most used, including those that format the font and adjust the overall appearance of the data available in the spreadsheet.

Clipboard

The first section of the Home ribbon features the *Clipboard* category. This collection of commands is the basic cut, copy, and paste functions that we typically use to make it easier to transfer, replicate, or remove data from different sources.

The small paint brush icon - called the *format painter* - isn't quite as familiar as the good ol' cut, copy, and paste, but it does serve an intuitive function. By using this feature, users have the option to copy the format used for a specific cell and then replicate it on another selection of cells.

For instance, if one cell is formatted with certain colors, borders, fonts, and alignment, selecting it using the format painter will copy those features and 'paste' them to the subsequently selected cell or group of cells to create a uniform appearance.

It's important to keep in mind however, that the format paste feature does *not* copy the contents of the selected cell. Instead, it only imitates the appearance of the cell. So, any of the data that's contained in the primary cell will not be replicated. To do this, users have the option to copy and paste data.

Font

In this category, MS Excel provides users the option to edit and customize the appearance of the font in each cell, as well as of the general appearance of the cell itself. The standard commands include *bold, italicize, underline, font, font size, cell fill color, font color,* and *cell borders.*

These are typically the most used commands in the entire user interface because they help make organizing data more overt. For instance, certain data can be color coded to make it easier for users to visually map out how each value relates to one another.

Changing the font styles and qualities can also give them a unique look compared to the rest of the data, serving the purpose of master headings for proper information division and categorization.

Later on, you'll learn how to make all of these custom qualities *conditional* - that is, they are displayed when cells meet certain criteria. For example, all cells with values *less* than the designated parameters will automatically display red cell borders to make them easier to spot in a spreadsheet full of data.

Alignment

The alignment features designate the positioning of the data relative to the size and space allowed by the cell. Data can be aligned to the top, middle, or base of the cell, and it can be aligned towards the left, right, or center.

Other than that, the alignment section also provides features that let users wrap the data or merge certain cells. Data can also be made to appear diagonal, vertical or horizontal.

These features might not seem quite as useful, but they do provide unique benefits in certain cases. For instance, 'wrapping' data in a cell prevents disrupting the rest of the spreadsheet's format.

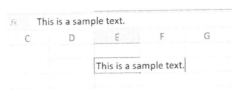

In this example, you can see that the text inside the cell under column E exceeds the space allowed by the cell. So, it goes beyond the cell and overlaps with the cell under column F.

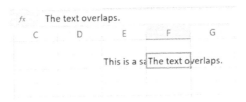

Once the cell under column F is designated its own content, then the data in the cell under column E is overlapped and unseen. Users have two options - they can adjust the width of the cell by changing the uniform width of the columns, or they can wrap the text.

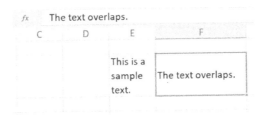

Shown here, the issue with the cell under column E was resolved by wrapping the text, which adjusts the height of the cell to accommodate the entire length of the text without it exceeding the width of the space. In the cell under column F, the text is accommodated by increasing cell width.

Merging cells on the other hand, is an essential feature for creating organized tables. This allows users to take numerous cells and turn them into a single cell with one designated value.

	A	B	C	D	E	F
1						
2			FIRST SEMESTER			
3		MONDAY	TUESDAY	WEDNESDAY	THURSDAY	FRIDAY
4	8:00 - 9 :00	ELECTIVE	SCIENCE	FREE	SCIENCE	ELECTIVE
5	9:00 - 10:00					
6	10:00 - 11:00	FREE	FREE	ENGLISH	ELECTIVE	MATH
7	11:00 - 12:00					
8	12:00 - 1:00	LUNCH				
9	1:00 - 2:00	MATH	FREE	MATH	ENGLISH	SCIENCE
10	2:00 - 3:00					
11						

Here, the user has merged certain cells to make an accurate representation of his or her schedule. The header 'First Semester' covers the entire selection of columns that represent days. Under each day, classes are merged to create a neat correspondence with their designated time. The designation for 'lunch' is consistent throughout the week, so merging the cells that represent that hour eliminates the need to write 'lunch' repeatedly throughout the days in the schedule.

The horizontal, vertical, or diagonal quality of data can also help make a messy spreadsheet much more organized. This can help save space and keep all the information needed within view without having to scroll away.

	A	B	C	D	E	F	G
1	1st Grading Period						
2	CLASS NUMBER	HOMEWORK 1	HOMEWORK 2	QUIZ 1	REPORT 1	PROJECT 1	HOMEWORK 3
3	1	98	92	96	89		
4	2	90	92	93	80		
5	3	91	94	88	91		
6	4	82	89	81	92		
7	5	83	88	81	93		
8	6	89	89	98	90		
9	7	87	80	90	91		
10	8	99	91	91	94		
11	9	98	92	92	90		
12	10	96	93	98	96		
13	11	93	90	90	93		
14	12	88	91	91	88		
15	13	81	94	82	81		
16	14	81	89	83	81		
17	15	98	88	89	98		
18	16	90	89	87	90		
19	17	91	80	99	91		
20	18	92	90	98	92		

In this example, an educator makes headers for quizzes, homework, and projects vertical in order to save space and ease the process of scanning grades. By doing this, students can get a clear picture of their academic performance by simply scanning the chart for the row of their grades. Had the teacher chosen to position the headers horizontally, it would end up looking like this.

	A	B	C	D	E	F	G
1				1st Grading Period			
2	CLASS NUMBER	HOMEWORK 1	HOMEWORK 2	QUIZ 1	REPORT 1	PROJECT 1	HOMEWORK 3
3	1	98	92	96	89		
4	2	90	92	93	80		
5	3	91	94	88	91		
6	4	82	89	81	92		
7	5	83	88	81	93		
8	6	89	89	98	90		
9	7	87	80	90	91		
10	8	99	91	91	94		
11	9	98	92	92	90		
12	10	96	93	98	96		
13	11	93	90	90	93		
14	12	88	91	91	88		
15	13	81	94	82	81		
16	14	81	89	83	81		
17	15	98	88	89	98		
18	16	90	89	87	90		
19	17	91	80	99	91		
20	18	92	90	98	92		

The wider spaces would have made it harder to view the grades accurately, since the format does cause some visual confusion. Condensing the data and limiting the spaces between numbers allows an easier viewing experience, and lets the user save space to eliminate the need to side-scroll when more information is added down the line.

Number

More often than not, MS Excel is used to organize and calculate numerical data, which is why the **number** category makes a practical addition to the home ribbon. This selection of features shows commands that let you customize the qualities of numerical data. It includes options that adjust the number of decimal places, apply a percent symbol to selected data, add commas, and a dropdown list selection that lets you designate numerical values as a specific format.

C6	⌄	Q fx	476.03
◢	A	B	C
1		January Report	
2	Period	Start date	Sales
3	1st week	1/1/2018	$433.35
4	2nd week	1/8/2018	$421.90
5	3rd week	1/15/2018	$398.12
6	4th week	1/22/2018	$476.03

In this example, you can see that the raw content of C6 according to the formula bar is '476.03'. However, since the cells under the header 'Sales' are formatted as *currency* values, MS Excel automatically adds the designated currency symbol before the numbers.

The benefit here is that for worksheets that use a lot of different kinds of numerical data, adding a currency symbol where appropriate will make it easier for viewers to see which cells contain values that represent money, and those that don't.

Why not just add the symbol manually? While that is absolutely possible, a manually added currency symbol could interfere with computations. For instance, if the user would like to add two currency values, or if the raw data includes a manually placed currency symbol, the computation would result in an error.

D2	⌄	Q fx	=B2-C2
◢	A	B	C	D
1				
2		450 $	398 $	#VALUE!

In this example, D2 comes up with an error when trying to subtract the contents of C2 from B2 because the dollar symbols have been added manually, interfering with the numerical values in the cells.

Styles

The styles command group lets you select a group of cells and change their appearance to display a uniform format. This is ideal for highlighting the boundaries of a table, and making your spreadsheet better suited to your personal preference.

The *conditional formatting* option lets you take a selection of cells and designate a style on those that meet certain parameters. This allows you to find specific outcomes especially if you've applied a formula across a large selection of cells.

For instance, a user hoping to put up a business might use this feature to determine the appropriate prices for the products and services offered by a future venture.

	A	B	C	D	E	F
1						
2		SERVICE	PROJECTED ASSOCIATED EXPENSES	CASH OUT PER UNIT	COST PER SALE	PROFIT PER SALE
3			Paint	$1.50		
4	1	Silkscreen t-shirt printing	T-shirt	$1.00	$20	($0.50)
5			Silk screen printing machine depreciation	$15.00		
6			Cleaning cost	$2.00		

36

In this sample computation for a silkscreen T-shirt printing service, the user has the option to move around the cost per sale in order to generate a sound profit. If each unit is sold at $20, then the profit for each sale would only total around $0.50. Unless the number under the 'profit per sale' column reaches the ideal amount, then the cells will continue to be red.

	A	B	C	D	E	F
1						
2		SERVICE	PROJECTED ASSOCIATED EXPENSES	CASH OUT PER UNIT	COST PER SALE	PROFIT PER SALE
3	1	Silkscreen t-shirt printing	Paint	$1.50	$25	$5.50
4			T-shirt	$1.00		
5			Silk screen printing machine depreciation	$15.00		
6			Cleaning cost	$2.00		

As the profit per sale exceeds $5.00, the red color is automatically lifted, and the cell shows the same format as the rest of the table. This makes it easy to spot when a value reaches a desired parameter, so you can adjust and tweak numbers without having to compute their viability each time.

The other two default functions in the styles category are *Format as Table* and *Cell Styles*. These choices provide users with pre-made table and cell designs to choose from, showcasing lots of different colorways that you can use to designate specific meanings, or to simply meet your own style preference.

Cells

The cells category lets you add cells, hide rows or columns, adjust their width or height, and organize your sheets. For instance, if you forgot to add a specific bit of information in an encoded group of data, you can add columns or rows to make it easier to add in what you've missed without messing up the rest of the table format.

	A	B	C	D	E	F	G
1							
2		SERVICE	PROJECTED ASSOCIATED EXPENSES	CASH OUT PER UNIT	OVERHEAD	COST PER SALE	PROFIT PER SALE
3			Paint	$1.50			
4	1	Silkscreen t-shirt printing	T-shirt	$1.00		$25	$5.50
5			Silk screen printing machine depreciation	$15.00			
6			Cleaning cost	$2.00			
7							

In this example, the previous table has been edited to include another column between 'Cash Out Per Unit" and 'Cost Per Sale.' Clicking the insert column feature automatically adds another column towards the left side of the active cell, making it easier for users to expand tables and information without disrupting the original format.

In the same way, users also have the option to delete columns and rows. This completely removes all the information and formatting that the cells might have contained prior to deleting. The name is retained and is designated to the cells to the right of the deleted column or to the bottom of the deleted row.

	SERVICE	PROJECTED ASSOCIATED EXPENSES	CASH OUT PER UNIT	OVERHEAD	COST PER SALE	PROFIT PER SALE
1	Silkscreen t-shirt printing	Paint	$1.50		$25	$5.50
		T-shirt	$1.00			
		Silk screen printing machine depreciation	$15.00			
		Cleaning cost	$2.00			

	SERVICE	PROJECTED ASSOCIATED EXPENSES	CASH OUT PER UNIT	COST PER SALE	PROFIT PER SALE
1	Silkscreen t-shirt printing	Paint	$1.50	$25	$5.50
		T-shirt	$1.00		
		Silk screen printing machine depreciation	$15.00		
		Cleaning cost	$2.00		

In this example, the column 'Overhead' was deleted. Its column title E was thus designated to the column to its right - 'Cost Per Sale', which was previously labeled column F.

Editing

The last category in the home ribbon is the *Editing* command group. In this category, you'll find the *Apply Total/Average, Autofilter, Clear Data, Sort or Filter Data,* and *Find and Select Data* features.

The apply total/average feature lets you generate the average of a set of data with a single click. If you have a list of numbers, placing your active cell at the bottom of it and then selecting the apply total option automatically calculates the average of the values in the column.

		SERVICE	PROJECTED ASSOCIATED EXPENSES	CASH OUT PER UNIT	COST PER SALE	PROFIT PER SALE
	1	Silkscreen t-shirt printing	Paint	$1.50	$25	$5.50
			T-shirt	$1.00		
			Silk screen printing machine depreciation	$15.00		
			Cleaning cost	$2.00		
			TOTAL	$19.50		

Here, the total $19.50 was arrived at by designating D7 as the active cell, and then clicking the apply total function. The program automatically selected all the numerical values that came after the header 'Cash Out Per Unit' and then adding them together using a *sum* formula. Users also have the option to do the same to produce an average.

The autofiller function on the other hand, lets you copy information from neighboring cells to the current active cell. The feature gives you the option to copy information from the cell above, below, towards the left, or towards the right of your active cell.

The sort data function lets you sort tabular information to make it easier to find the least and greatest values. This can be particularly beneficial if you need your data presented in an ascending or descending order, depending on your needs.

Finally, the find and select data feature lets you locate specific values based on what you search. For instance, if you need to find all the students who scored 95 and above on an exam, using the find and select data option can ease the process of locating them in an extensive table of information.

The Insert Ribbon

The *Insert Tab* is the second one available on the default Excel interface. Here, users are given the option to add a bunch of information using different formats and coming from different sources.

Tables

The tables command category provides users two options - pivot table and table. The table option is pretty much self-explanatory and provides a very straightforward method for users to define the boundaries of a specific table throughout a worksheet.

The pivot table, on the other hand, is an intuitive feature that makes it easier to understand data. It helps increase the significance of information and lets users extract precise data from a more extensive collection of values also present on the Excel workbook.

⬚	A	B	C	D	E
1	RECIPIENT	DATE	ITEM	TYPE	COST
2	Miller	1/14/2017	Apples	Wholesale	$890
3	David	1/18/2017	Oranges	Retail	$200
4	Miller	2/25/2017	Bananas	Retail	$178
5	Willis	2/13/2017	Cauliflower	Wholesale	$1,203
6	Willis	2/16/2017	Cauliflower	Wholesale	$920
7	Garcia	3/4/2017	Bananas	Retail	$190
8	David	1/29/2017	Apples	Retail	$86

Here, we have a partial table from a vegetable and fruit wholesaler/retailer. He has a few customers, some of whom are repeat buyers. The information in his table includes the name of the buyer, the date the items were sent, the item, the type of sale, and the cost of the transaction.

If this vegetable and fruit seller were to extend his table by adding more information, it can be difficult to find certain data because of the number of factors included. Using a pivot table can make it easier to filter just the information you need so you don't need to go back and forth through an extensive table looking for specific data.

To create a pivot table, simply select the option from the Insert ribbon. A pop-up will appear prompting the user with the next step. This includes selecting where the data will come from (including external sources), the range of the table if it exists in the present worksheet, and where you want the pivot table to appear - the current worksheet or a new one.

Now that you've chosen the source of your data, click OK and a new pane appears. This pivot table pane is where you get to choose which headers you want to include and how they should appear in your new pivot table.

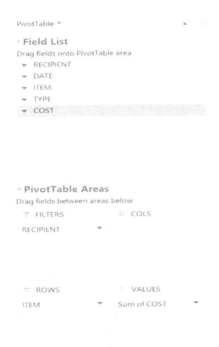

Here, you can see that the user has selected these headers to include in the pivot table. The result looks something like this:

9	RECIPIENT	(ALL)	▾
10			
11	ITEM	▾ Sum of COST	
12	Apples	976	
13	Bananas	368	
14	Cauliflower	2123	
15	Oranges	200	
16	Grand Total	3667	

All the items are presented with a sum of their total cost. Users have the option to filter the recipient to show the items that were shipped to him only. The items can also be filtered to show just specific items the user wants to see. For instance, if you'd only like the pivot table to display the sales made to Miller, click the drop-down arrow and select Miller from the list. It should look something like this:

9	RECIPIENT	Miller	▾
10			
11	ITEM	▾ Sum of COST	
12	Apples	890	
13	Bananas	178	
14	Grand Total	1068	

Now, the pivot table will only present the items purchase by Miller as well as the sum of the cost of those purchases. If the user would like to see only specific items sold to all the individuals in the list, the table allows the option to filter items as well. For instance, if you'd only like to see apples and oranges, clicking the drop-down arrow next to the item header and filtering the choices to show only apples and oranges will come up with this table:

9	RECIPIENT	(ALL)	▼
10			
11	ITEM	T. Sum of COST	
12	Apples	976	
13	Oranges	200	
14	Grand Total	1176	

The pivot table obviously offers some incredibly helpful uses to Excel spreadsheet users who want to be able to see their data in a more intuitive light. These tables can be edited and adjusted to function in a variety of ways, making data analysis seamless and effortless.

In the same way, adding a table from the insert ribbon also offers a unique experience compared to data that's just manually encoded. For reference, let's look back at the original table for fruit and vegetable sales:

	A	B	C	D	E
1	RECIPIENT	DATE	ITEM	TYPE	COST
2	Miller	1/14/2017	Apples	Wholesale	$890
3	David	1/18/2017	Oranges	Retail	$200
4	Miller	2/25/2017	Bananas	Retail	$178
5	Willis	2/13/2017	Cauliflower	Wholesale	$1,203
6	Willis	2/16/2017	Cauliflower	Wholesale	$920
7	Garcia	3/4/2017	Bananas	Retail	$190
8	David	1/29/2017	Apples	Retail	$86

Here, you can see that data is merely presented without giving the user any options for optimal viewing. Perhaps for smaller tables, this wouldn't be a problem. But if you're handling a lot of information and you need to be able to see specific values based on your purpose, it's ideal that a table provides you some features for better viewing. Using the table option located in the insert ribbon will help make your table a little more intuitive.

	RECIPIENT	DATE	ITEM	TYPE	COST
1	RECIPIENT	DATE	ITEM	TYPE	COST
2	Miller	1/14/2017	Apples	Wholesale	$890
3	David	1/18/2017	Oranges	Retail	$200
4	Miller	2/25/2017	Bananas	Retail	$178
5	Willis	2/13/2017	Cauliflower	Wholesale	$1,203
6	Willis	2/16/2017	Cauliflower	Wholesale	$920
7	Garcia	3/4/2017	Bananas	Retail	$190
8	David	1/29/2017	Apples	Retail	$86

Here, the user has converted the standard data into a spreadsheet table. Doing this made the information stand out against the rest of the white worksheet space by adding colors. It also made drop down arrows appear beside each header name. This allows a more intuitive experience, allowing you to filter certain data to see information more accurately.

For instance, if you'd like to see only the wholesale transactions, click on the drop-down arrow beside the TYPE header and filter the selection to display only wholesale transactions.

	RECIPIENT	DATE	ITEM	TYPE	COST
1	RECIPIENT	DATE	ITEM	TYPE	COST
2	Miller	1/14/2017	Apples	Wholesale	$890
5	Willis	2/13/2017	Cauliflower	Wholesale	$1,203
6	Willis	2/16/2017	Cauliflower	Wholesale	$920

It should give you something that looks like this. Now, the table only shows all the wholesale transactions by temporarily hiding the other rows that don't meet the criteria. This can be done for any of the headers, so you can filter information and display only the values that are necessary at the moment.

For those who are a little more visual, there is the pivot chart option. This generates a separate chart on top of the pivot table that was presented earlier. The purpose is to give users a clear visual representation of their data for even more intuitive viewing.

Moving around the filters on the pivot table will consequently change the appearance of the table to reflect the data that's currently presented on the pivot table. This is an indispensable tool for individuals giving reports, or for those who simply want a clear visual representation of numerical data.

Illustrations

The second category in the insert ribbon is the illustrations group. Here, users have the option to add images, shapes, clipart, and smart art to their file. Images that have been saved to the computer can be added to the spreadsheet by clicking the insert image option. The clipart option lets users choose from a variety of graphics that are present in the MS Office database. More graphics can be found by connecting to the internet.

Shapes on the other hand are exactly what they seem.

These are a variety of shapes including arrows, speech and thought bubbles, equation shapes, and flowchart shapes that can be used to add a touch of creativity and visual appeal to your Excel spreadsheet.

Here, a plus shape has been added between two headers to make the spreadsheet a little more attention grabbing. There is also smart art available which is basically a collection of different flowchart formats that let users present information in a creative and interesting way. The smart art formats can be used to show organizational structure, processes, cycles, and lists to name a few.

Charts

Excel data can be used to generate charts within the file. These can be particularly ideal if you plan to present your report to another individual, since it gives you better material that's easier to explain. Charts can be generated by selecting data from the current worksheet, and then choosing the kind of chart you want to use.

Excel offers users a variety of chart layouts, including bar graphs, line graphs, pie graphs, area charts, and scatter charts, to name a few.

Text

The text category under the insert ribbon offers users the capability to insert text boxes, headers and footers, word art, signature lines, objects, and symbols into their spreadsheet. While these functions are rarely ever used in Excel, they can be ideal for those who want to create visually stimulating layouts that encourage viewers to engage with the spreadsheet more intently.

The Page Layout Ribbon

The page layout ribbon is commonplace for all MS Office programs. This tab contains features and options that allow users to format the 'page' so that it meets their preferences if and when the spreadsheet is printed. The category includes options like themes, margins, scale, and visibility of gridlines and headings when printing.

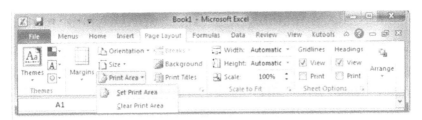

For the most part, this section of the program pretty much explains itself since it's present across all other MS Office software.

The Formulas Ribbon

The formulas ribbon is where things get a little messy. This category is where users will find most of the unique features offered only by MS Excel, making it one of the more technical areas of the entire software.

First, we'll start with the basic option - *insert function.* Upon clicking this feature, users are prompted with a pop-up. The default functions are featured at the start, and these include IF, SUM, AVERAGE, COUNT, MAX, SIN, and SUMIF.

The IF function is one of the most used in the entire Excel program. It allows users to apply a logical test so that a cell will display a specific value if that test is satisfied. If it isn't, then the cell will display what the user designates as the result if the value if false.

For example, a teacher wants her spreadsheet to show whether a student has passed or failed based on the final grade listed in column A. Then she can apply a logical test to help make it easier to see which students have failed her class.

	A	B	C	D	E
1	PRELIM	MIDTERM	FINAL	GWA	PASS/FAIL
2	89	70	76	78.33	PASS
3	87	90	89	88.67	PASS
4	88	87	90	88.33	PASS
5	90	81	93	88.00	PASS
6	91	80	88	86.33	PASS
7	80	71	70	73.67	FAIL
8	94	80	90	88.00	PASS
9	70	73	72	71.67	FAIL

In this example, she designed a table that would automatically compute the General Weighted Average of each student based on the grades she inputs from the prelim, midterm, and final period. Then, the spreadsheet would automatically display whether a student passed or failed based on the number generated under the GWA column. How was she able to do this?

E2			f_x	=IF(D2<75,"FAIL","PASS")		
	A	B	C	D	E	F
1	PRELIM	MIDTERM	FINAL	GWA	PASS/FAIL	
2	89	70	76	78.33	PASS	

In the formula bar, you can see the IF statement she wrote in order to display pass or fail. The logical test states IF cell D2's value is LESS THAN 75, then the active cell should display the word "FAIL". However, IF D2's value is GREATER THAN 75, then the active cell will display "PASS".

When it comes to the IF statement, the possibilities are endless, and users can even add new IF statements into existing IF statements to expound the possible outcomes they might see if certain criteria are met.

fx   =IF(D2<75,"FAIL",IF(D2<=99,"PASS",IF(D2=100,"EXCELLENT!")))

In this expounded IF statement, the user has added another outcome aside from simply pass or fail. If students manage to come out with a GWA of 100, the spreadsheet will display "Excellent!" Scores between 99 and 75 receive a "Pass", and those below 75 are marked "Fail".

Another function used commonly in Excel is SUM. Essentially, this function lets you total a list of numbers together. The active cell where the formula is added will display the total of the numbers in the selected range.

fx	=SUM(D2:D9)
C	D
	# ITEMS
	100
	89
	90
	93
	88
	70
	90
	72
	692

In this example, the user has totaled the numbers under the # ITEMS header using the formula =SUM(D2:D9). The cell reference numbers in the parentheses represent the range where the numbers to be totaled should be sourced.

On top of that, users also have the option to expound the SUM formula by adding other features to it. The standard equation symbols - such as +, -, ×, and ÷ - can also be included at the end of the formula depending on the outcomes you need.

So, for example, a user can add a subtraction clause at the end to deduct a number of items that perished in transit. So, the formula would look something like:

fx	=SUM(D2:D9)-5	
C	D	E
	# ITEMS	
	100	
	89	
	90	
	93	
	88	
	70	
	90	
	72	
	687	

The function that calculates average works in a similar way to the sum function. The only difference of course is that after it calculates the sum of the numbers, it also divides the total by the number of variables in the range. The count function lets users figure out how many variables are present. So, it essentially *counts* the number of cells with viable content.

The SUMIF function is similar to the SUM function, with the exception that it lets users designate specific criteria. For instance, if a user wants to collect the sum of just a specific value within a given list of values, they can set that as their designated criteria. So instead of getting the total of all the numbers in a range, the software will only get the sum of the values that meet the chosen parameters.

The Excel software has an extensive function library that features a number of different categories where you can find all of the available formulas on the program. The categories include financial, logical, text, date & time, lookup & reference, math & trigonometry, and other functions. Exploring these libraries to learn more about what you can do with Excel can help enrich your user experience.

Defined Names

The software provides users the chance to create their own *defined names* within the spreadsheet. This function helps improve efficiency so that you can keep referencing variables that might be regularly used within your file. With a defined name, you can replace the variables in a formula using the name you've given a specific cell or range of cells.

Formula Auditing

The formula auditing category features functions that help users determine whether they've used their formulas the right way. This process of auditing makes it easier to spot where errors might have occurred so that users can address problems to come up with more accurate results.

Tracing precedents on a cell with a formula will show you all the cells that are involved in that specific formula. Tracing dependents on a cell will show you which cells with formulas use the contents of your active cell as part of their equation.

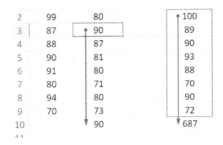

2	99	80	100
3	87	90	89
4	88	87	90
5	90	81	93
6	91	80	88
7	80	71	70
8	94	80	90
9	70	73	72
10		90	687

In this example, the value '90' in the last cell of that column is a dependent of the value '90' in the 3rd row. On the rightmost column, the values in the blue outlined area are the precedents of the value '687' in the 10th row in the column. To remove the arrows, users simply need to click the remove arrows option in the same category.

The show formula button temporarily changes the perspective of the file to show you not the answers to the formulas you've input, but the formulas themselves.

2	99	80	100
3	87	90	89
4	88	87	90
5	90	81	93
6	91	80	88
7	80	71	70
8	94	80	90
9	70	73	72
10		=MAX(B2:B9)	=SUM(D2:D9)-5

So, in this example, when the show formulas button is activated, it displays two formulas present in the worksheet. Upon deactivating the function, the program will display the values that result from the formula.

Calculation

By default, MS Excel is programmed to automatically calculate values after you've input your formulas. If you choose to turn off automatic calculation, then you can use the calculate options at the end of the formulas ribbon to execute formulas once you're finished inputting them.

The Data Ribbon

The data ribbon is where users can seek out data sources from different locations other than just the Excel workbook. This ribbon tab also offers features that remove duplicate information in tables and lists of data. Perhaps the most useful feature in the entire ribbon however is the "What If Analysis" option.

This function lets you try different variables for your formulas, so you can see the possible outcomes and errors. Trying out your formula with this function before actually executing it in the sheet will help guarantee that you don't end up with seemingly correct calculations that don't accurately reflect what you're trying to come up with.

The Review and View Ribbons

The review and view ribbons - much like the page layout ribbon - are mainstay categories in all other MS Office programs. These ribbons include functions that let users review the document and add comments, which can be necessary when reviewing work submitted by another individual.

The view ribbon simply offers a number of features that change the way you see your file. Here, you can activate or deactivate gridlines, headings, the formula bar, and the task bar to name a few. On top of that, users also have a choice to switch between different views such as full screen, reading layout, and page break view.

- QUIZ BREAK -

Let's take a quick refresher quiz to see how well you understood the topics in this section. Answers to this quiz (and the others that follow) can be found at the end of the guide.

1. What is the area of the worksheet where you can access a few commands that are most commonly used. This can be found at the upper righthand corner of the program and aligns with the title of the file.

2. What are the DEFAULT ribbon tabs that MS Excel displays for its users?

3. TRUE OR FALSE: When you click on a cell that contains a SUM equation, the formula bar will display the ANSWER to that specific equation.

4. You entered text into a cell and it exceeded the width of the column. To have all the information fit neatly into the cell's size, what should you do? A) adjust the column width, or B) wrap the text.

5. TRUE OR FALSE: Deleting column B will cause the contents of column C and all other columns after it to move one column to the left - so the contents of column C would now be labeled column B.

6. Which ribbon can you find the option to create a pivot table?

7. Which ribbon tab would you choose if you want to

hide the gridlines of your file?

8. You have one column of numerical data. You want to figure out which ones exceed the value of 50 and have decided to do this by using an IF statement. If the cell exceeds 50, then the result should be "Yes". If not, it should display "No++". How would you write your IF statement?

9. TRUE OR FALSE: When you trace precedents, you're looking for the values that a formula needs as part of its equation.

10. You want to find out how your formula will perform when applied to certain values in your file. What would be the best function to use to determine the viability of a formula?

Chapter 3 - Formatting Your Excel Spreadsheet

In the corporate world, the attention people have for business presentations is dictated by how visually stimulating these reports are made. So, if you're planning on having a few others look into your Excel spreadsheet, you might want to incorporate a few design hacks to make them more appealing.

Fortunately, Microsoft knows just how important design can be and they try to make it easy for everyone - even those with minimal design experience. That's why they offer a variety of set templates and themes that you can choose from to help liven up your spreadsheets with little to no effort.

A lot of the formatting commands can be found in the home ribbon under the format category. The cell style option shows users a variety of colors and styles they can use to draw attention to singular cells or a range of selected cells. For the most part, these style options were designed to make specific data stand out, such as a final annual value for sales.

Under the page layout ribbon, there are also a variety of formatting commands. These change the color palette of your file, and even allow you access to different themes that add a touch of personality to your spreadsheets. Choosing a specific theme changes the default colors available for fonts, highlights, and other text features in the font category of the home ribbon.

Basic Features for a Visual Spreadsheet

You don't really need to do too much in order to get your spreadsheet to look visually stimulating. For starters, the borders feature can add a touch of personality to your spreadsheet while adding emphasis to necessary components of your data.

Excel offers a variety of border styles and weights, so you can use them to draw attention to cells that are of particular importance. They also come in handy when presenting tables in a spreadsheet as they delineate where a table starts and where it ends.

Other ways to highlight the boundaries of your table would be to use the format as table function. Here, users will find a variety of table styles and colorways that can be used to automatically edit and personalize a selected table section. Colors are dictated by the currently selected theme, so changing the theme can give you access to more colorways.

Keeping it Visual with Charts

Adding charts into your Excel spreadsheet can be highly beneficial to your viewers because it adds context to your data, and makes sense of otherwise mundane or even boring numerical values.

Just like any other MS Office program, Excel offers a variety of charts that you can use to visually represent your data. Each one however, has an ideal purpose, so they can't necessarily be used interchangeably.

- **Pie charts** - Show parts of a whole. Ideal for presenting how a single value or entity is divided into parts.

- **Bar graphs** - Represent a comparison of values between different variables, allowing viewers to clearly see which are higher or lower.

- **Line graphs** - Used to show an ascent or descent of values over time. For instance, line graphs can be used to represent the fluctuation of sales over a 12-month period.

- **Scatter charts** - Dots are used to represent unique values or occurrences. These values don't necessarily need to correlate, thus the lack of any sort of connection between the scattered points.

Charts can be fun to work with when you're trying to make your Excel spreadsheet more dynamic. And aside from that, they're fairly easy to work into your file.

To insert a chart into your spreadsheet, visit the insert ribbon tab and select the chart style that would work best for your purpose. Once you've chosen your chart, a new tab called "Chart Tools" will appear at the end of the ribbon tabs. Here you can find functions that can help customize the way that your charts or graphs appear.

If you didn't select a range of data to use for your chart prior to choosing your chart style, or if you want to change the data it uses, you have the option to do so under the chart tools ribbon tab. Simply click the command and select the range of data within your spreadsheet to update the information in your chart.

Chapter 4 - Getting Efficient with Excel

Windows is all about making things easier for their users. That's why they pride themselves in their capacity to develop user-friendly interfaces and software commands that help their patrons learn to become more efficient with their programs.

All throughout any Windows or Microsoft environment, you're bound to encounter shortcuts. These keyboard combinations are used to simplify the process of enacting certain commands so you don't have to swim through toolbars and ribbons in search of those functions.

The Most Common Excel Shortcuts

The Excel program is no stranger to shortcuts. The software features a unique set of keyboard commands that a user can leverage to help speed up the process of getting work done.

F2

Edit active cell. This key lets you type into the active cell more readily, since there are some instances when simply typing straight into your keyboard without

EXPERT @ EXCEL: FOR BEGINNERS

activating the edit mode first might interfere with cell content.

For instance, if a cell has an *existing* formula then typing straight into your keyboard will overwrite its contents. Pressing F2 first will bring your active cell into edit mode, so that you can edit the information it already contains.

F4

Pressing F4 will repeat the last edit that you performed. This helps save time if you want to re-paste a formula or text.

CTRL + ALT+ F9

If your worksheet has automatic calculation turned off, pressing CTRL + ALT + F9 will calculate all the worksheets currently open.

F11

Pressing F11 will prompt the user to create a new chart. Simply highlight the information you want to include in your chart, and then press F11. A new chart with all the pertinent information will be automatically generated to eliminate the need to have to search through the software's native toolbars.

ALT

When you press ALT, you'll see a number of different letters appear along the toolbars and tabs that are present in the software. Clicking on the letters that correspond to each one can shorten your navigation through the ribbons and give you access to special functions without having to remove your hands from the keyboard.

ALT + =

This shortcut will automatically calculate the sum of a group of data. Note that the active cell should be placed directly under the data to be totaled before pressing the ALT + = shortcut.

ALT + Enter

Pressing ALT + Enter will start a new line in your current active cell. The cell will then be automatically adjusted in terms of row height to accommodate the extra line.

ALT + H + O + I

Working as a sequence, this command lets you auto-size your columns to accommodate the information expressed in its cells. Press first the ALT button and the H key to navigate to the home tab. While maintaining the ALT key, press O which moves you to the format menu. Once that's done, press I to automatically adjust the width of the columns.

CTRL + `

This command displays all the formulas present in your worksheet. So instead of showing the results of the formulas you've keyed in, the file will reflect the actual formulas.

CTRL + Backspace

If you've got an extensive spreadsheet and you navigated too far from your active cell, you can navigate back with this shortcut. Press CTRL and backspace and the program will bring you back to your current active cell.

CTRL + Shift +

This command changes your date format to the default day, month, year. It can be used on cells that contain data regarding dates.

CTRL + K

This prompts the user with a pop-up that lets them insert a hyperlink into their file.

CTRL + Shift + $

If you have one active cell, or if you've selected a range of cells, executing this shortcut will automatically convert the values in your chosen cell or cells to currency format.

CTRL + Shift + &

This combination of key presses will automatically apply a border to the cells selected. If there are no selected cells, then the command will add a border to the active cell.

CTRL + B

As part of standard Microsoft Office practice, CTRL + B makes the selected text bold. It can be applied to numerous cells at once.

CTRL + I

CTRL + I italicizes information displayed in a specific cell. Users also have the option to italicize numerous cells at a single time.

CTRL + U

Pressing the CTRL + U combination underlines the information in a range of cells or the active cell, depending on which the user has selected.

CTRL + X

Cutting information from MS Excel can be done by executing the shortcut CTRL + X. Once the data is cut, it is copied to the clipboard and kept there until new information is copied or cut. Data that has been cut will be removed from its original place in the file.

CTRL + C

The difference between cutting data and copying data is that the latter *does not* remove the original data from its source. The command CTRL + C simply copies existing information and leaves the original text or data where it was taken from.

CTRL + V

Once information is placed in the clipboard - either by cutting or copying - users then have the option to paste it. Executing this shortcut will paste the most recently cut or copied content to the selected destination in your file, represented by the active cell. Data can be virtually pasted without limitations, as long as there's enough space on the worksheet to accommodate it.

CTRL + A

This shortcut selects all of the information in a given field. If the active cell is placed within a table, pressing CTRL + A will select all of the contents in that specific table only.

CTRL + F

This shortcut results in a pop-up screen where users can input keywords to find specific information in their worksheet.

CTRL + H

Unlike the find function, the CTRL + H function leads users to the find and replace feature. This simply means that once the document searches for the data that meets the user's parameters, they're given the option to replace all of the search results with new data.

For instance, if a user accidentally inputs the wrong name repeatedly, using the find and replace feature can help locate all the erroneous names and replace them with the correct spelling.

This is not an all-inclusive list. Microsoft programs are highly extensive and there are hundreds upon hundreds of shortcuts that you can use to ease the entire process of using the software and speed up your work. You can learn more about these shortcuts by exploring your MS Excel program or by looking them up on the web through the Microsoft Help Center.

Keep in mind however that with Excel's Visual Basic feature, you can have the option to designate your own shortcut keys that you can use within the Excel environment. Designating a shortcut key combination to your own unique action sequence can make it easier to accomplish certain tasks and relieves the repetitiveness that most numerical processes require.

Tread lightly, though - there are literally *hundreds* of pre-programmed commands. So, before you designate a shortcut key combination to your specially designed macro, make sure you consider those that are already programmed into the software. If you make the mistake of designating your sequence on a shortcut command that already exists, you can overwrite that specific pre-programmed shortcut.

- QUIZ BREAK -

Answer with either the shortcut command or the function of the given shortcut keys.

1. CTRL + A

2. Automatically apply a border to the selected cells.

3. F2

4. F4

5. Start a new line in a cell.

Chapter 5 - Of Macros and Visual Basic

If you're just learning the ropes of Excel, you might find your brows furrowing and your concentration completely fixed on all the different variables you need to take into account. However, as you become more accustomed to the platform, you might find the entire process of editing, customizing, and calculating data a little repetitive - especially if there are certain tasks you need to do repeatedly.

Enter *macros*. Designed to help ease the process of repetitive tasks, macros in Excel are essentially recordings of your keystrokes and mouse clicks, creating a sequence that you can repeat over and over again with minimal effort. This helps reduce the time you spend performing the same process and allows a more efficient workflow.

The Basics of Creating Macros

By default, the Excel program will only show you the basic ribbon tabs included in the discussion we shared a few chapters back. So, to be able to access the function of creating macros, you need to first activate the *Developer ribbon*.

To do this, right click anywhere on the active ribbon - it doesn't matter which ribbon is currently active - and select the option "Customize the Ribbon..."

Once you've chosen to customize the ribbon, a dialog box will appear. If you can't see the option to add new ribbons, select "Main Tabs" from the customize the ribbon drop down list in the dialog box. This then shows you the different ribbons you can add to your default list.

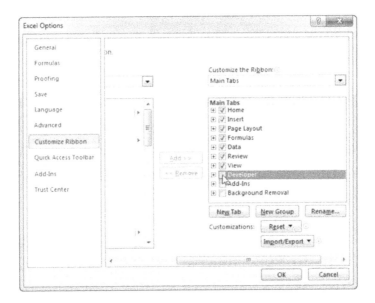

Tick the "Developer" option from the list and click OK to save your changes. You should now be able to access the developer functions on your Excel spreadsheet, next to the View ribbon tab.

Here you'll find the basic functions you need in order to create a 'mini-program' within MS Excel. However, before you begin recording your macros, there are a few things you need to keep in mind.

- Macros are recordings of your clicks and key strokes. It doesn't record the time you take in order to perform the next action, and instead simply records the sequence of the actions as you do them.

- More often, your macro will need a reference point. Consider this the starting point of the series of actions which will guide the macro as to the location of the other data that it needs to handle.

- You can record more than one macro and save them to your macro list. This allows users to stow away a variety of unique functions that can be used for repetitive tasks.

To start, select your active cell. This should be the starting point of your sequence which should help the macro determine where it should begin the process if you choose to utilize it again later on.

	A	B	C	D	E	F	G	H	I
1									
2	COPY	SUM		PRODUCT		COPY	SUM		PRODUCT
3		91					537		
4		875					128		
5		356					3		
6		24					64		
7		4					342		
8		26					18		
9			42					42	
10									

In this example, the macro will:

1. Take the sum of the numbers in column B, to be displayed in cell B9.

2. Multiply the result by the number in cell C9.

3. The product will be displayed in cell D9.

4. This final answer will then be copied to cell A9.

To complete this sequence, first choose your active cell or starting point. In this case, it's cell B3 - the starting number in column B where the numbers will be totaled.

Once it's highlighted as the active cell, go to the developer ribbon and click "use relative references." Now you're ready to record your macro.

Upon clicking the record macro button, a dialog box

will pop up asking you to give your macro a name and to add a short description as to what it does. Keep in mind that macro names can't have spaces. Users also have the option to designate a shortcut key if they see it necessary.

Designating a key to your macro means you can repeat that sequence of steps at any point in your worksheet by simply executing your chosen shortcut. It's important to note however that you need to make sure your chosen shortcut combination doesn't already exist as it is possible to overwrite them. So, you should be careful to designate any of the shortcuts that are installed into MS Excel by default.

Once you click OK, Excel will start recording your actions. Considering the sequence example above, the user would first have to get the sum of the numbers in column B, multiply that number by the value in C9 and display their product in cell D9, before copying that final digit in cell A9.

Here's what it should look like once it's done:

	A	B	C	D
1				
2	COPY	SUM		PRODUCT
3		91		
4		875		
5		356		
6		24		
7		4		
8		26		
9	57792	1376	42	57792

Once the sequence is completed, go back to the developer tab and click stop recording. You now have your new macro. To test it, start a new collection of data in the same formation and then go to your available list of macros.

Choose the macro you recorded and click run to perform the sequence on the new block of data. If it works properly, it should automatically complete the steps in less than a second's time.

	A	B	C	D	E	F	G	H	I
1									
2	COPY	SUM		PRODUCT		COPY	SUM		PRODUCT
3		91					537		
4		875					128		
5		356					3		
6		24					64		
7		4					342		
8		26					18		
9	57792	1376	42	57792		45864	1092	42	45864

In this example, the data starting from column F to I was calculated using the macro that was recorded with the first set of numbers.

Macros can be particularly useful for processing a large quantity of information. These small programs within a program can accomplish a series of steps for you, saving your time and eliminating the need to perform everything manually.

Essentially, every function on you can perform with MS Excel can be recorded and turned into a macro. So, the possibilities are endless when it comes to this highly intuitive Excel feature.

If you decided to designate a shortcut key combination to your macro, then you can skip going through the developer ribbon, macro list, and run macro sequence to enact your special series of actions. Simply choose your active cell and execute your shortcut command to start your macro sequence without having to click through the menu choices.

Visual Basic for Beginners

Because of its highly programmable and versatile nature, MS Excel makes an excellent introduction to programming. This programming environment lets you edit areas of preselected sections of a code so that you can generate a program that suits your needs. The developer tab in the Excel ribbons should give you access to your VBA functions.

Currently, VBA is considered obsolete in the world of programming lingo. However, it does offer users the capability to adjust and adapt their MS Office programs to serve them a variety of functions that would otherwise be unavailable to most.

Most of the VBA benefits can be explored by inserting controls into the document. Things such as buttons, drop down lists, check boxes, and scroll bars, to name a few, can all be coded with VBA language in order to add another facet of functionality to your entire Excel workbook.

What is the real-life application of VBA? As previously mentioned, VBA is running behind other programming languages in our current time. So aside from being able to adapt your MS Office programs, there's very little that you can do with VBA. The language itself can't be used to code applications and it can only be accessed through an operating MS Office software.

So, what's the point of learning an obsolete language? Coding can be very confusing. If you dive right into those more complicated languages, then you might find yourself throwing in the towel before you're able to learn how to manipulate an action button. Learning the basics with VBA can help hone your skills and makes a great stepping stone towards further learning.

- QUIZ BREAK -

Enumerate the steps to recording a macro, considering that the Developer ribbon has not yet been activated on your standard Excel ribbon tab collection.

Conclusion

There's a whole lot to learn and a whole lot to love about MS Excel. Even with just its basic functions, you can get a whole lot more out of the user experience, enriching your Excel files and giving you an edge over the other guys at work.

Of course, it's not the simplest thing to learn. With branches that stretch out into programming, it can be a bit of a challenge to make full sense of MS Excel especially if you're not completely knowledgeable about how all those different commands and features work.

Fortunately, this quick guide has been of some assistance. With these essentials, you've got everything you need to get the best of MS Excel and make the most of each and every spreadsheet you create.

Don't be afraid to explore MS Excel as you continue to learn and master these basic skills. There's a world's worth of advantages to the software, and they're all just waiting for you to master them.

So, whether it's for something as personal as your own household finances, or something as large-scale as a year-end company report, remember to pull up that spreadsheet and wow people with your excellent Excel prowess.

Quiz Answers

QUIZ 1

1. Quick access toolbar

2. Home, Insert, Page Layout, Formulas, Data, View, Review

3. FALSE

4. Both A or B

5. TRUE

6. Insert

7. Page Layout

8. =IF(CELL<50, "No", "Yes") OR =IF(CELL>50, "Yes", "No)

9. TURE

10. What If Analysis

QUIZ 2

1. Select all

2. Ctrl + Shift + &

3. Edit active cell

4. Redo

5.Alt + Enter

QUIZ 3

Right click anywhere on the active ribbon > Customize the ribbon > tick 'Developer' box under the Main Tabs selection > Decide on your macro sequence > select the active cell that will work as a reference point > click Use relative references > click Record macro > choose the name for your macro > start the action sequence > click Stop recording once done.

Expert @ Excel

Pivot Tables

A Step By Step Guide To Learn And
Master Excel Pivot Tables To Get
Ahead @ Work, Business And
Personal Finances

Chapter One: Overview of PivotTables

Introduction

A pivot table is an essential tool/program in data exploration and analysis because it helps the user to manipulate the data efficiently to suit his/her needs. It entails summarizing data to a new table from another table. The primary operations that can be applied during this process include; data sorting, averaging or summing data into the first table typically by grouping. It is possible to explore, track and analyze thousands of data with the help of a small flexible table that helps you analyze different perspectives of your data.

Main features of pivot tables include:

1. It is easier and straightforward to create pivot able hence save time

2. Allows you to create reports instantly

3. Enables the user to create interactive reports which can synchronize with the audience

4. You can quickly mix the data by merely dragging fields, sorting and performing different calculations on the data.

5. A pivot table allows you to have the best presentation of the data

6. You can create multiple reports from the same pivot table instantly.

As we move on, you will understand how this features in details and how they function, with time, you will have a concrete knowledge concerning the pivot tables.

The History of Pivot Tables

Bill Jelen and Mike Alexander refer to Pito Salas as the father of pivot tables in their book "Pivot Table Data Crunching." Salas noted that spreadsheets have data patterns while he was working on a new program that eventually became to be known as *Lotus Improve,* https://en.wikipedia.org/wiki/Lotus_Improv. He thought that a tool that could aid users to recognize the patterns mentioned above would help in building more advanced data more quickly. By using the "Improv" tool, users had an opportunity to define and store sets of data categories and the change the view of the data simply by dragging the category name using the mouse. This core function would end up providing the model that is now applied in pivot tables. A few months after the release of Improve in 1991, "Brio Technology" published *Macintosh Implementation* that was called *DataPivot,* but the technology was implemented in 1999.

In early 1914 Microsoft excel en.wikipedia.org/wiki/Microsoft_Excel came up with "PivotTable" and was introduced in the market. This tool was later improved to the modern version of Excel. In 2000, excel introduced *pivot charts,* a tool that can represent "pivot table" data graphically.

Mechanics of Pivot Tables

When you enter data in excel, it appears in flat tables; this means that they consist of only of columns and rows, for example, the following portion of a spreadsheet shows a sample data.

	A	B	C	D	E	F	G
1	Region	Gender	Style	Ship Date	Units	Price	Cost
2	East	Boy	Tee	1/31/2005	12	11.04	10.42
3	East	Boy	Golf	1/31/2005	12	13	12.6
4	East	Boy	Fancy	1/31/2005	12	11.96	11.74
5	East	Girl	Tee	1/31/2005	10	11.27	10.56
6	East	Girl	Golf	1/31/2005	10	12.12	11.95
7	East	Girl	Fancy	1/31/2005	10	13.74	13.33
8	West	Boy	Tee	1/31/2005	11	11.44	10.94

A table such as this one contains many data items and at times it can prove too problematic when you want to summarize the data and generate reports. With the help of a pivot table, you can quickly summarize this data to get the desired information. There is no limitation on the usage of the pivot table; you can use it in any situation as far as it deals with data.

Typically, a pivot table is composed of the row, column, and data field; the column is the "ship" date, the row the "region" and the data is represented in "units. These fields allow you to perform several kinds of operation such as sum, average, count, and standard deviation among others.

Implementation of Pivot Tables

Different from other excel tools, pivot tables are not created automatically, in the Microsoft, for instance, you must first select the entire data in the original table and then insert tab to select the pivot table. You have the option to add the pivot table into the already existing sheet, or you can create a new spreadsheet to co contain the pivot table. The user is provided with the pivot table, which has the column headers in the data. You will see more about the pivot tables as we proceed on the "create" a pivot table part.

The Pivot Table Layout Design

The layout design for the pivot tables has got four options as shown below

Date of sale	Sales person	Item sold	Color of item	Units sold	Per unit price	Total price
10/01/13	Jones	Notebook	Black	8	25000	200000
10/02/13	Prince	Laptop	Red	4	35000	140000
10/03/13	George	Mouse	Red	6	850	5100
10/04/13	Larry	Notebook	White	10	27000	270000
10/05/13	Jones	Mouse	Black	4	700	3200

Report filter

This option is used to apply a filter to the whole pivot table. For instance, if the color of the item field is dragged and dropped in this area, the build table will contain the filter above the table. The report filter comprises *drop down* options such as as *black, white, red* among others. When you select an option from the list of drop-down options, for instance, let's say green, then, the data that displayed will be only the one from the rows that have color green.

Column labels

This feature is used to apply filters to the columns that have to be displayed on the pivot table. For example, if the field containing *the salesperson* is dragged and dropped into this area, then the pivot table created will include values from the "salesperson" column. Besides, the *total* column will be added.

For instance, by using the table above, this action will generate five columns in the pivot table. One column will be for each salesperson and the *total* column. A filter will appear above the data and on the *column labels* from which the user can now select the *sales person* to be presented in the pivot table. Note that the pivot table created will have no numerical values because no data has been inserted so far. However, when the data is selected, the values will automatically update in the *grand total* column.

Row labels

Row labels are used to apply filters to the rows that will be displayed on the pivot table. Let's say for example that the *salesperson* field is dragged into this area, the table that will be built after that will contain values from 'salesperson'. That is, the table will have the number of rows that equals the number of "salesperson," the *total* row will also be added. Using the above sample table, this command will automatically create five rows in the table. The rows will be for each salesperson and the Grand Total.

Above the data, on *Row Labels*, a filter will appear from which the user can choose one *sales person* to feature in the pivot table. Again, the table will have no numerical data because it has not been selected. However, when the numerical field is selected, the values will update automatically on the "Grand Total" Row.

Summation values

Summation values usually take a field that contains numerical values that can be used to carry out various calculations. However, using text values it doesn't mean that it is wrong, but instead of a sum, it will give a count. So in the sample table provided above, if the "units sold' field is dragged and dropped in this area together with the row label of the "salesperson," the instructions will lead to the generation of a new column, *sum units sold*. This column will show values against each *salesperson*

Four Main Areas of a Pivot Table

Pivot Table Areas Diagram

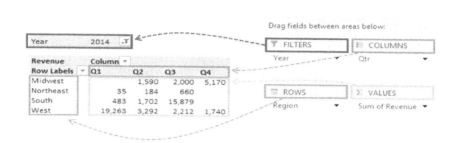

Values area

This area is large rectangle shaped that is below and to the right of row and column headings. The values found in the value area are the calculations of the data. Primarily, the data that you drag to the values area is the data that you are interested in measuring, for example, revenue, count of units and the average price.

Row area

The data placed in the row area field shows the display of unique values from that row all the way down to the left side rows of the table. In most of the time, the *row area* has one filed, but in some cases, there might be no fields at all.

Column area

This area is comprised of the headings that run down the pivot table. This area gives you the column-oriented perspective. When you place data in one of the column areas, the unique values from that column are displayed in a column-oriented perspective. Besides, the column area is ideal for showing the trend over time or creating a data matrix.

Filter area

This is an optional area that can be formed at the top of the pivot table. In the case of the table presented above, the filter area is comprised of the region filed; the pivot table is designed to show all parts. Besides, this area enables the user to apply filters to the pivot table with much ease. Based on your selections, you can efficiently use filters to the reports generated from pivot tables. However, the type of data that is mainly included here is the one that you want to separate from others so that you can give them specialized focus. For example, you can use a line of business in a particular region and employees. Follow this link for more details on the pivot table layout design.

Chapter Exercise

1. What do you understand by the term excel pivot table, what are some of the essential points you have noted about excel?

2. Did you know about Excel pivot tables before this tutorial? I you did what did you know about them?

3. If you add either new rows or new columns to the pivot table source data, the pivot table is not updated even when you click on 'Refresh Data.' Why and what is the solution?

4. By any means can you repeat 'row headings' in the Pivot Table?

5. Is it possible to show the text in the data area of the Pivot Table?

6. What are the features that make pivot tables an excellent tool to work with on excel?

7. Can you briefly describe how the pivot tables function?

8. Give the layout design of excel tables and give an elaboration of each area and why it's important, what can happen if it's omitted?

9. Describe the main areas of a pivot table and how any manipulation of one area affects the others?

10. Do you need technical skills to work with Excel pivot tables?

Chapter Two: When to Use Pivot Tables

The pivot table presents the dimensions for a measure of columns and rows. It allows you to analyze data through the use of different standard and sizes at the same time. The dimensions determine how the data in the pivot table will be grouped.

The pivot table is mainly useful when you want to include different measures and dimensions on the same table. Besides, it is also useful when you want to restructure them for various reasons.

1. When you want to summarize data like for example finding the average sales for each region for each product from the product sales data table

2. When you want to introduce a unique value in any of the columns in the table

3. In case you want to make a dynamic pivot chart, pivot table will help serve you a great deal.

4. In case you want to filter, sort and drill down data in the reports without writing the formulae.

5. A pivot table is also useful in case you want to link data sources that are outside excel and produce reports out of such data

Chapter Exercise

1. Apart from the uses mentioned above of pivot tables, can you think of other applications?

2. How can you link data from sources outside the excel spreadsheet to your pivot table?

3. When would be the appropriate time to use Excel pivot tables?

4. Why are pivot tables more preferred over the excel spreadsheets?

Chapter Three: Working With Excel Pivot Tables

You can create a pivot table from a range of data, or you can use the excel table. You can also start with an empty table so that you can key in your data when you are sure as to what you are looking for. If this does not sound like a good option for you, you can still use the pivot tables recommended by excel. Excel recommended pivot tables can give you a clue on the pivot table layout that is the best for summarizing your data.

Excel offers you a more powerful approach of developing pivot tables from multiple tables, unique data sources as well as external sources of data. The power pivot works on its database referred to as the data model.

But before we move to the creation of the pivot tables, you need to have a deeper insight into the usual pivot table before dealing with the complicated pivot table.

Fields and Areas of Pivot Table Layout.

The layout of the pivot table depends highly on the fields that you select for your report and also how you arrange them in areas. The selection is just simple; you can do it by dragging the fields until you realize the results that you desire. During the dragging of the pivot table fields, the pivot table instantly adjusts accordingly.

Discovering Data with the Pivot Table

The primary aim of using the pivot table is to explore data thoroughly to extract significant information. You can achieve this action through the use of several options that includes but not limed to, sorting, filtering, nesting, collapsing, expanding among others.

Summary of Value

After collecting the data that you require through the use of a variety of techniques, the next step to take is summarizing the data. Summarizing the data is quite simple because Excel provides you with a variety of techniques that you can apply to synthesize the data to suit your requirements. Besides, you can switch across different types of calculations to test the results. This activity will take just a few seconds of your time.

Keeping the Pivot Table Updated

After exploring and summarizing the data, you have to repeat the process in case you have updated your data source. After you have done that, you can now refresh the pivot table so that it can reflect the updated data.

Reports Generated by Pivot Tables.

You need to present your data as a report after summarizing it. The reports generated through the pivot tables are collaborative in nature, in that, even a person who is not familiar with excel basics can also use these reports. Due to its dynamic nature, these reports enable the user to modify the reports quickly to reflect the kind of details that you want to focus on that are of interest to your audience. Besides, you can also structure the pivot table report to feature both the standalone presentations and the needs of an integral report or any other case that you might be looking to accomplish.

How to Use the Pivot Table Function

The pivot table function is the most widely used feature in Microsoft Excel. Furthermore, this feature allows you to visualize data from different perspectives to get a deeper insight. You are on the right platform if you have never built a pivot table or you are seeking to sharpen your skills.

	A	B	C	D	E
1	Sales Person	Territory	Sales	Commisions	
2	Lacy	Northeast	$ 11,206	$ 1,681	
3	Gerard	Central	$ 6,164	$ 616	
4	Tony	Northeast	$ 5,260	$ 526	
5	Jennifer	Central	$ 7,555	$ 755	
6	Frank	Southeast	$ 4,413	$ 441	
7	Wesley	Southeast	$ 4,549	$ 455	
8	Frank	Southeast	$ 5,400	$ 540	
9	James	Northeast	$ 4,829	$ 483	
10	Patrick	Southeast	$ 4,690	$ 469	
11	James	Northeast	$ 14,877	$ 2,232	
12	James	Northeast	$ 7,681	$ 768	
13	Gerard	Central	$ 12,995	$ 1,949	
14	Diane	West	$ 9,737	$ 974	
15	Clark	West	$ 13,214	$ 1,982	
16	Lacy	Northeast	$ 5,550	$ 555	
17	Tony	Northeast	$ 12,048	$ 1,807	
18	Frank	Southeast	$ 4,027	$ 403	
19	Jennifer	Central	$ 6,499	$ 650	
20	Lacy	Northeast	$ 13,283	$ 1,992	
21	Patrick	Southeast	$ 12,006	$ 1,801	
22	Hanna	Northeast	$ 12,943	$ 1,941	
23	Wesley	Southeast	$ 8,731	$ 873	
24	Jennifer	Central	$ 14,283	$ 2,142	
25	Wesley	Southeast	$ 4,152	$ 415	

The above diagram shows a simple data set, but it is good enough to work with. One thing to note is that all rows cannot fit in this column, what if there were more columns? You can filter data in this table, but pivot table can make things more efficient. Check the following process on how to construct a pivot table.

Chapter Exercise

1. What are the different options that you can use to create functional excel pivot tables?

2. After you have created the pivot table, what are the factors that determine the layout of your pivot table?

3. What do you understand is the primary aim of using pivot tables instead of just using the normal excels spreadsheets?

4. Describe the fundamental actions that help you to work with pivot tables, especially modifying the data contained in pivot tables?

5. Describe you can update excel pivot table and how you can maintain it updated?

6. Data summarizing is one of the factors that makes excel pivot tables very popular, why can't just use another tool to summarize your data?

7. What is the nature of the reports created by excel pivot table?

Chapter Four: Building Excel PivotTables

You can create a pivot table either from the excel table or from other data sources; the key thing is that, whatever the source you use, the header for the columns should be placed on the first row of the data. In case you are sure about the fields that should be included in the pivot table, you can establish your data from scratch. But if you are not sure about the best layout to use, use the recommended pivot table by excel and choose the one that best suits your data needs.

The First Step towards Creating a Pivot Table

The first thing you need to do is to ensure that there are no blank rows in your source data. Having empty cells will cause you problems.

	A	B	C	D	E
1	Sales Person	Territory	Sales	Commision	
2	Lacy	Northeast	$ 11.206	$ 1.681	
3	Gerard	Central	$ 6.164	$ 616	
4	Tony	Northeast	$ 5.260	$ 526	
5	Jennifer	Central	$ 7.555	$ 755	
6	Frank	Southeast	$ 4.413	$ 441	
7	Wesley	Southeast	$ 4.549	$ 455	
8	Frank	Southeast	$ 5.400	$ 540	
9	James	Northeast	$ 4.829	$ 483	
10	Patrick	Southeast	$ 4.690	$ 469	
11	James	Northeast	$ 14.877	$ 2.232	
12	James	Northeast	$ 7.681	$ 768	
13	Gerard	Central	$ 12.995	$ 1.949	
14	Diane	West	$ 9.737	$ 974	
15	Clark	West	$ 13.214	$ 1.982	
16	Lacy	Northeast	$ 5.550	$ 555	
17					
18	Tony	Northeast	$ 12.048	$ 1.807	
19	Frank	Southeast	$ 4.027	$ 403	
20	Jennifer	Central	$ 6.499	$ 650	
21	Lacy	Northeast	$ 13.283	$ 1.992	
22	Patrick	Southeast	$ 12.006	$ 1.801	
23	Hanna	Northeast	$ 12.943	$ 1.941	
24	Wesley	Southeast	$ 8.731	$ 873	

For instance, the blank row in the above spreadsheet would cause you problems when you are creating the pivot table. You need to make sure that the spreadsheet consists only of the adjusting data. To remove the blank row, you need to go to home menu, click find, then special, blanks and finally delete rows.

After making sure that your data is uniform, click on any of the cells in the spreadsheet containing your data, then click 'insert' tab. While still there, find 'tables' then click pivot table. Create a pivot table wizard will appear automatically.

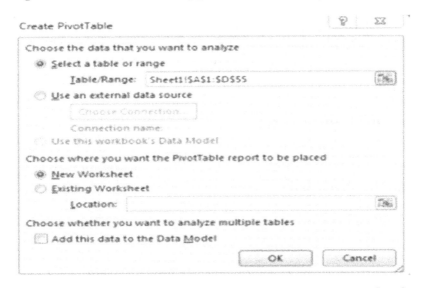

The pivot table pre-selects the data and will also display the range of the data at the top place of the wizard. Nevertheless, you can adjust this setting if you don't like it but the source data is in the adjacent range, there is no need to change anything. And this is the advantage of making sure that there are no blank spaces in the spreadsheet cell to make sure the source data display the way it is supposed to be. Having accomplished the above process, leave the pivot table placement option on the default 'New Worksheet' then click OK.

Excel will automatically open a new worksheet and place the pivot table there, below is a sample of what you should expect though they might not look quite alike.

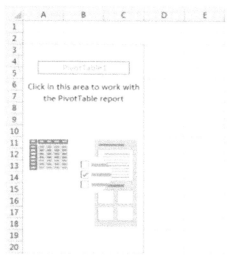

In this blank slate is where you will find the pivot table fields and the four areas we mentioned previously where you could place them. If you do not see something like the sleet below, click on the pivot table found on the left side of the same worksheet.

If you still cannot locate the pivot table fields, check on the 'show' group of the analyze tab to select the 'field list.' By clicking on the field list, the background becomes dark grey.

Feeding Data into the Pivot Table

After you have successfully created the pivot table, you are now ready to go into the real practice of working with the pivot tables. For example, drag the *sales person* from the 'field list' and transfer it to the rows.

Automatically, rows form on the blank pivot table. Let's try to drag the sales value to the value area.

Now you can see that it's possible to view the sales totals by sales person very quickly and without complications.

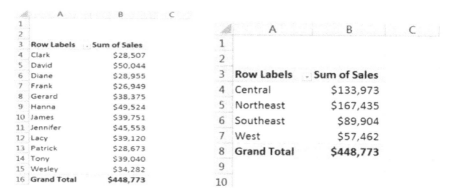

This is a great way to visualize the data, but there are more possibilities. Let's say you want to drag total sales by this territory. We can do it by removing the *sales person* from the *rows area* and drop territory there. The following visualizations will appear

Again, when you drop the salesperson under territory in the rows area, the display you get becomes even more meaningful.

Row Labels	Sum of Sales
Central	$133,973
David	$50,044
Gerard	$38,375
Jennifer	$45,553
Northeast	$167,435
Hanna	$49,524
James	$39,751
Lacy	$39,120
Tony	$39,040
Southeast	$89,904
Frank	$26,949
Patrick	$28,673
Wesley	$34,282
West	$57,462
Clark	$28,507
Diane	$28,955
Grand Total	$448,773

If you happen to click on the minus (-) sign, found on the left of the territory labels, you can end up collapsing the list. You will still get the same visualization that you had before varying the sales rep. Besides, you can also filter on a specific row, for instance, you want to view something specific. You have to go for the down arrow, row labels auto filter, uncheck all the boxes except the ones you have created.

Techniques for Advanced Visualization

Let us now try and move the *territory* to the *filters* area and see what will happen. In the values area, it will also alter the sales for the commission.

	A	B	C
1	Territory	(All)	
2			
3	Row Labels	Sum of Commisions	
4	Clark	$3,511	
5	David	$6,372	
6	Diane	$2,896	
7	Frank	$3,350	
8	Gerard	$5,068	
9	Hanna	$6,897	
10	James	$5,337	
11	Jennifer	$5,779	
12	Lacy	$5,136	
13	Patrick	$3,468	
14	Tony	$5,100	
15	Wesley	$4,087	
16	Grand Total	$57,002	

It is possible to select the commissions by the sales representative for any territory. When you filter on the central, it allows you to sift through each set of sales in each territory efficiently. You can also filter the rows with the help of the row labels.

Settings for the Value Field

The most critical trick to use when working with pivot tables is the ability to change the value field setting. It is straightforward to do the changes, you have to click on the down arrow on the right side of the values area, and a value setting box will appear automatically.

On this box, you can change how you want the summary of your values to appear, then turn the setting to average and click okay.

	A	B	C
1	Territory	Central	*x*
2			
3	**Row Labels**	**Average of Commisions**	
4	David	$1,274	
5	Gerard	$1,267	
6	Jennifer	$1,156	
7	**Grand Total**	**$1,230**	

Alternatively, you can still perform the same action by right-clicking on the column in the pivot table, then go to summarize values by. Select count if you want a quick tally on the number of sales per each sales representative.

⬛	A	B	C
1	Territory	(All)	▼
2			
3	Row Labels	Count of Sales	
4	Clark	3	
5	David	5	
6	Diane	4	
7	Frank	4	
8	Gerard	4	
9	Hanna	5	
10	James	4	
11	Jennifer	5	
12	Lacy	5	
13	Patrick	5	
14	Tony	5	
15	Wesley	5	
16	Grand Total	54	

There is also an essential feature, 'show values as.' You can change the values back to the sum of sales, but you need to make sure that the territory filter is set to 'all.' After verifying that, right click on any column in the pivot table and choose 'Show values as'

You should be following all the different options closely we are elaborating on how you can apply the pivot table and deal with your data more efficiently. Let us now choose a column total; you will be able to see all the sales by representatives representing the percentage of the total sales.

	A	B	C
1	Territory	(All)	
2			
3	Row Labels	Sum of Sales	
4	Clark	6.35%	
5	David	11.15%	
6	Diane	6.45%	
7	Frank	6.01%	
8	Gerard	8.55%	
9	Hanna	11.04%	
10	James	8.86%	
11	Jennifer	10.15%	
12	Lacy	8.72%	
13	Patrick	6.39%	
14	Tony	8.70%	
15	Wesley	7.64%	
16	Grand Total	100.00%	

The last stage, move to the column area. First of all, you need to move back to the territory filed from the filters area to column. Automatically, we get a new visualization of the data. All the options that we have mentioned including this ones show just an example of the flexibility of the pivot tables to enable you to summarize, format and display your data the way you want.

	A	B	C	D	E	F	G
1							
2							
3	Sum of Sales	Column Labels					
4	Row Labels	Central	Northeast	Southeast	West	Grand Total	
5	Clark				$ 28,507.0	$ 28,507.0	
6	David	$ 50,044.3				$ 50,044.3	
7	Diane				$ 28,955.0	$ 28,955.0	
8	Frank			$ 26,949.3		$ 26,949.3	
9	Gerard	$ 38,375.5				$ 38,375.5	
10	Hanna		$ 49,524.0			$ 49,524.0	
11	James		$ 39,751.5			$ 39,751.5	
12	Jennifer	$ 45,552.8				$ 45,552.8	
13	Lacy		$ 39,119.6			$ 39,119.6	
14	Patrick			$ 28,672.5		$ 28,672.5	
15	Tony		$ 39,039.9			$ 39,039.9	
16	Wesley			$ 34,282.1		$ 34,282.1	
17	Grand Total	$ 133,972.6	$ 167,435.0	$ 89,905.9	$ 57,462.0	$ 448,773.4	

Now we have come to the end of how you can create pivot tables on the excel spreadsheets and how they function. It is more efficient to analyze and generate reports on pivot tables based on the nature of your data. Besides, you have seen how simple it is to get started with pivot tables and how they help you to visualize your data in different ways.to get more information on pivot tables visit,

https://excelwithbusiness.com/product/pivottable/

Chapter Exercise

1. What are the things you need to consider before embarking on the construction of pivot tables?

2. What are the steps you need to follow to build a functional pivot table?

3. What are some of the problems that you might encounter while creating the pivot tables in case your source data contains blank cells?

4. How do you remove the empty data cells in the source data for your pivot table?

5. How do you change the values setting in the pivot table?

6. Upon refreshing a Pivot Table, it always loses the formatting like the column width. How can this be corrected?

7. Is it possible to adjust the default summary function for data from COUNT to SUM?

8. When linking to a pivot table cell, a GETPIVOTDATA formula is created. How would you avoid this?

9. How would you enable automatic refresh in Pivot Table upon opening the workbook without using macros?

10. Can you hide the error values in the data field of Pivot Table? If yes, how?

Important Points to Note about Pivot Tables

Experts in excel state that pivot table is the most excellent and perfect tool to work with on excel if you want to get quality results from your data and save time as well. Not any other tool in excel that can give you the flexibility and data analytical power like the pivot table do. I don't object to this statement; I support it 100%. Excel pivot tables are sturdy and fun to work with. The following are some of the tips you should grasp about excel pivot tables;

It can only take less than a minute to create pivot points. There is a held notion that building pivot tables are a complicated process and time-consuming, this is not true. If you compare the time you will take to prepare reports, and by using pivot tables, you would never think of going manual again, pivot tables are incredibly fast.

Chapter Five: The Various Function You Can Undertake Using The Pivot Tables

It is quite exciting and fun when you use the drag option to change fields on the pivot table and sit back as you watch excel doing the magic and give different representations of your data. However, you can find yourself falling into problems very quickly if you are not keen on the action that you are carrying out. You might command some options that will entirely alter your data and not be able to turn back.

Before you start doing anything on the pivot table, make sure that you have a solid plan to follow. Understand what you are trying to measure and sketch some simple reports that will help you determine whether you are on the right track or you have lost it all. Besides, the sketchy notes will guide you through the many options that you might be considering executing. Keep it simple and focus on the data you want to measure and the results you are aiming to achieve.

Use the Pivot Table to Create a Dynamic Range of Data

When you use the excel spreadsheets for the source data you want to use in the pivot table, you will get enormous benefits. Pivot table makes your data range 'dynamic.' Dynamic range means that the scale of the table will expand and shrink automatically when you remove or add data to the table. This means that you don't have to worry that your table is missing some data, no; every detail of your data will be displayed. Beside the pivot table is always in sync with your data.

To use the pivot table;

1. Chose any cell in the data and use CtrL-T shortcut on the keyboard and create a table

2. Click the option; summarize with pivot tables

3. Construct the pivot table normally

4. The data you add on the table will appear automatically on the pivot table

Counting Items Using the Pivot Table

The pivot table is designed to count any text field by default. This is an advantageous and essential feature in business operations. For instance, let's say you have some employees and you want to get a count per department. To get a break down to every department, you can follow the following steps.

1. Create the pivot table the usual way by following the steps we mentioned earlier

2. On the row label, add the department

3. On the value area, add the employee Name

4. The pivot table will automatically display the count of employees per department

Check the spreadsheet below as a sample of what to expect

Breakdown of employees per department

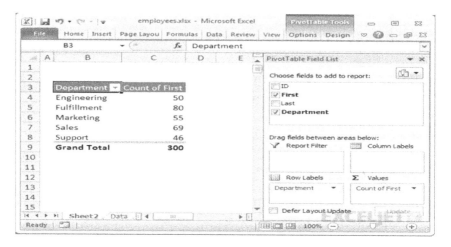

How to Show Totals Regarding the Percentage

When it comes to working with pivot tables, many people prefer displaying results concerning percentages rather than count. For instance, let's say that you want to show the breakdown of sales per product. Instead of showing the total sales per product you want to display the percentage sale of the entire product sales. Let's assume that in your pivot table you have created a field that you have named sales in your data; you have to follow the following steps to show the percentage of the total sales.

1. On the pivot table add the product as the Row Label

2. On the value area of the pivot table, add sales

3. Then you right click on the sale field and set show values as "to % of the total"

See the illustration below on how you can show the percentage

count of your data

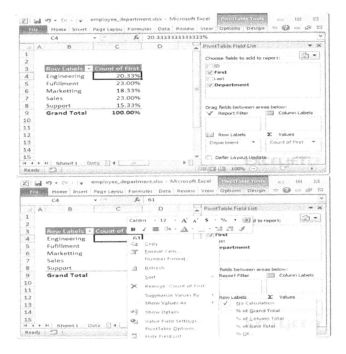

You can Use the Pivot Table to Create a List of Unique Values

A pivot table is efficient in finding the exceptional value in the fields because pivot table is designed to summarize the data. This is an excellent method that allows you to see all the value in the field and will enable you to locate errors and other variations in the data. Again, let's assume that you have sales data and you are interested in seeing the list of sold products. The following are the steps that can help you create the product list.

1. Create the pivot table

2. On the row label, add the product

3. You can add any category you want in the value area, maybe category or the customers.

4. After you have followed the above steps correctly, the pivot table will display the list of all the products contained in the sales data.

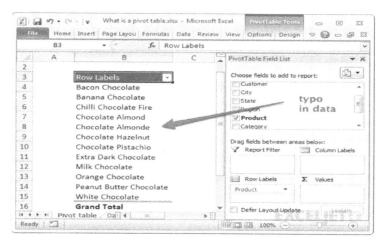

Follow this link to view the video tutorial on how to create a unique list of values https://exceljet.net/core-pivot

Self-Contained Pivot Table

After you create the pivot table from the data contained in the same excels spreadsheet, it is possible to remove the data from the pivot table, and it will still remain functional even without the data. The reason behind this abnormal behavior is that the pivot table has a unique feature knows as "pivot cache" that is responsible for maintaining the exact duplicate of the data created in the pivot table.

1. You need first to refresh the pivot table to ensure that the cache is updated

2. Delete the worksheet that contains the data

3. After that you use your pivot table normally

Check out how you can make a self-contained pivot table from this link https://exceljet.net/tips/how-to-make-a-self-contained-pivot-table

Grouping the Pivot Table Manually

Primarily a pivot table groups the data automatically in many ways; it's not a must that the pivot tables have to group the information automatically. You can also do it manually, into your customized groups. For instance, let's assume that you already have a pivot table that contains the breakdown of employees per department. Let's say that you want to go further and classify them in their respective departments such as fulfillment, finance, marketing, IT into group one and engineering and PR in group two. The two groups, 1& 2 does not appear in your data, they are the custom groups that you have created. To group your data in the pivot table into such grounds, follow these steps.

1. Click control and then select the items in the first group one by one

2. On one of the items, right click and from the menu that is displayed, choose the group

3. Excel will create a new group and name it group one

4. On column b select sales and marketing and name it as you did above

5. Excel will form another group and call it group two

Check the example below

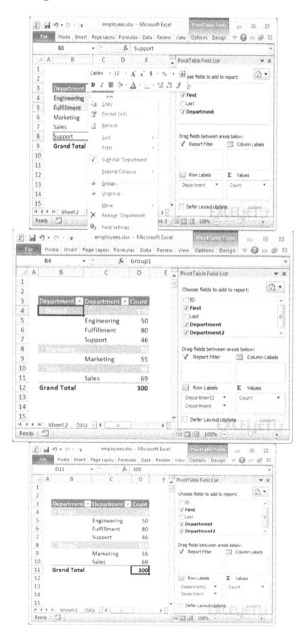

Cloning the Pivot Tables just in Case you need Another View

When you have one set of the pivot table, you might not be satisfied because you want to have a different view of the same data. Don't worry, with excel pivot table, almost every activity you want to carry out in excel is possible. You can adjust the existing pivot table to create the view you want. But if you are generating a report than that you aim to be updating it on an ongoing basis, the easiest way to go about it is clone the table. When you do the cloning, you get the view of data from both sides.

There are two ways that you can clone the pivot table. Both methods are easy; it depends on the one that interests you. The first method entails duplicating the worksheets containing the pivot table. Right-click the worksheet tab and copy it in the same workbook. The other method that you can employ is by copying the pivot table and pastes it into another location. By using these two approaches, you can create as many copies as you want.

The advantage of cloning the pivot table using the above two methods is that the pivot tables that you copy share the same pivot cache. This implies that, when you refresh one of the copy clone or the original pivot table, all the related tables will be restored too.

How do you Unclone a Pivot Table to Refresh Independently?

Situations might change and force you to want to unclone the pivot tables that you had cloned before. This might occur in case you want to modify one of the clones, but you don't want the change to affect the original pivot table. For instance, let us say that you grouped a date field in one pivot table clone, after refreshing, you discover that you had accidentally grouped the same date field in another pivot table that you had no intentions of changing or whatsoever. What you need to understand is that pivot tables share the same field groupings as well as a cache when they are cloned.

To avoid frustrations and regrets, the following is a procedure on how you can unclone the pivot table to institute changes to an individual clone. It means that you have to unlink it from the pivot cache that it shares with other clones in the same spreadsheet.

1. First, cut the pivot table to the clipboard

2. Then paste it into a new workbook

3. Refresh the pivot table

4. After you have done refreshing, paste it back to the original workbook

5. Do away with the temporary workbook

After following the above steps correctly, the new pivot table will have no links to other pivots; you can then modify it the way you want.

How to Do Away with the Unwanted Headings

The default layout for new pivot tables is compact; it displays the *row labels, column labels* in the pivot table. These headings are not the most intuitive especially to the people that do not make use of the pivot table when working with excel. There is an easy way that you can do away with these headings if you find them too odd, switch the pivot table layout to outline or tabular layout from a compact design. This action will make the pivot table display the actual field names the pivot table is supposed to have, the shading are much more sensible. In case you want to get rid of all these labels at once, look for *the field headers button* on the analyze tab found on the pivot table tools ribbon. Once you click this button, all the headings will be disabled entirely.

Check the following illustration.

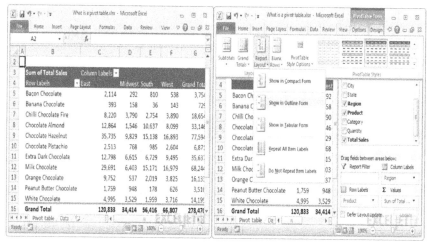

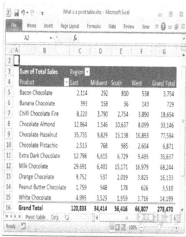

Pivot Tables Allow you to Turn Off Auto Fit when Necessary

A pivot table is designed in such a way that when you refresh it, columns containing data adjust automatically to fit the data. At times this is a good future, but it can prove to be challenging especially if you have other things you are working on in the same worksheet or you had adjusted the pivot table widths manually, and you don't want them changed. However, it is easy to disable this feature, right-click inside the pivot table and select, 'pivot table options.' In the box displayed, unmark the "auto-fit column widths on the update." Check the example below

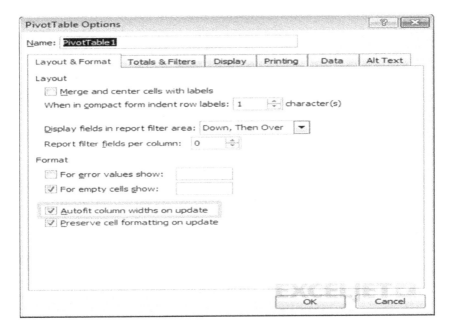

Chapter Exercise

1. Which 3 report formats for Pivot Tables are available in Excel 2007 or later?

2. How can you disable automating sorting in Pivot Tables?

3. How do you check whether a Pivot Table is modified?

4. Which option is used to add column(s) in Pivot Tables to compute the values in run-time?

5. What is the difference between Pivot Charts Vs. Regular Charts?

6. What is a Pivot Cache?

7. Can you make a Pivot Table from multiple tables?

8. How can you show totals in terms of percentage on pivot table?

9. How do you create a list of unique values using the pivot table

10. What do you understand by the term "dynamic range of data"?

11. How can you remove data from the pivot table and still maintain it to be functional?

12. What factor makes it possible to transfer data from the pivot table and still remain functional?

13. What is a pivot table and the various methods you can use to clone the pivot table?

14. Indicate the different roles that pivot tables help you to carry out?

15. What can you do to view the data displayed on the pivot table in different dimensions?

Chapter Six: Benefits of Using Pivot Tables

This section is meant for those of you who don't get what it is all about with pivot tables. Maybe you have ever tried the pivot tables once, and you did not see the big deal with them because you did not know how to work with them and you ended up a frustrated user. Don't worry sometimes they can be that way if you don't have the knowledge required to use them.

If you use excel and you don't use the pivot tables for one or two reasons, or you don't get as to why you should use them where's the excel spreadsheet can serve you perfect alone. Below are the reasons why you should start working with pivot tables.

Pivot Tables are incredibly fast

It is true that you can build the summary of the data you want manually if you have the formula to do it and generate reports manually. However, despite how smart and fast you think you are, it will cost you a lot of your time. For instance, in his book, "Excel 2013 Pivot Table Data Crunching". Mr., Excel Bill Jelen using his expert skills in excel, he managed to create a manual summary of products sales by region. He stated that it took him 77 keystrokes and if you can pull this in ten minutes time, then you should consider yourself an excel guru. He then contrasted the time he took to generate the report manually with pivot table approach. With only a few clicks, the work that he spent a lot of time doing was done. This proves that, no matter how fast you think you are in excel, the pivot tables will always beat you to nil regarding speed and competence.

You Don't Require Formulas in Pivot Tables

Yes, that is right; a pivot table does not need you to insert any equations so that it can analyze your data. You can build a pivot table with only a click of the mouse and drag option. To show how sturdy the pivot table is, this can be illustrated below. Let's for instance group all order in the sales data to see the breakdown of small sales and large orders

Order Value	Total Sales	Order count
$ 1.00	$ 3	3
$ 1.25	$ 10	8
$ 1.50	$ 2	1
$ 1.75	$ 2	1
$ 2.00	$ 10	5
$ 2.50	$ 23	9
$ 3.00	$ 15	5
$ 3.75	$ 4	1
$ 4.00	$ 28	7
$ 4.50	$ 5	1
$ 5.00	$ 55	11
$ 6.00	$ 96	16
$ 6.25	$ 19	3
$ 7.00	$ 84	12
$ 7.50	$ 60	8
$ 8.00	$ 96	12
$ 8.75	$ 140	16

In the above worksheet, there is just too much data to work with; however, we can request excel to group the order in the groups of $100. When you click okay, a new layout will appear that does the grouping perfectly, check the table below

Order Value	Total Sales	Order count
<100	$ 98,010	2106
100-200	$ 77,634	567
200-300	$ 33,643	141
300-400	$ 16,948	49
400-500	$ 9,682	22
500-600	$ 6,118	11
600-700	$ 2,643	4
700-800	$ 5,201	7
800-900	$ 5,977	7
900-1000	$ 1,896	2
>1000	$ 20,720	12
Grand Total	$ 278,470	2928

The summary that has been generated above shows that out of 3000 order, 2106 of the orders are less than $ 100 and the orders that have the value higher than $1000 are only 12. Just imagine the kind of a formula that could have been required to create this report manually. It cannot even be easy due to a lot of calculations involved. You cannot understand it even if you succeeded to generate the report manually. Pivot tables remain your perfect tool when you are working with excel data.

Elimination of Mistakes

In most times, people are always worried that their worksheets could contain errors. Or at one time you prepared the report manually, and the management noticed some mistakes in the formula that you used, it's such a bad experience. But you are not alone, these kinds of errors occur all the time even to the excel gurus. However, you can eliminate those frustrations and lack of credibility by merely using the pivot tables. There is no chance of messing up in pivot tables because no formula that is required, your role is only to make sure that the source data is correct. No matter the size of the data you are dealing with, excel handles 100% of the calculations and formatting and your results will be perfect

Pivot Tables Make You Look Like an Expert

You must have noticed by now that formatting excel content is tricky and the same time is very time-consuming. To make matters worse, if a client or the boss wants the work to be configured differently, you need to go back to square one and start afresh. You will never go wrong with pivot tables, all the formatting applied is automatic and you have the chance of presenting professional work to your boss. To emphasize on that point, have a look at the following report that has been prepared by pivot table.

Customer	Product	2011	2012	2013	Grand Total
Agnes Whole Foods		1008	1386	1483.5	3877.5
	Bacon Chocolate	34	36	38	108
	Chilli Chocolate Fire	118	250	138	506
	Chocolate Almond	23	154	218	395
	Chocolate Hazelnut	455	257.5	480	1192.5
	Chocolate Pistachio		129.5		129.5
	Extra Dark Chocolate	220.5	339	280.5	840
	Milk Chocolate	88	20	218	326
	Orange Chocolate	37.5		66	103.5
	White Chocolate	32	200	45	277
Crazy Oats		16330	16708.5	18653	51691.5
	Bacon Chocolate	288	20	266	574
	Banana Chocolate	45	27.5	25	97.5
	Chilli Chocolate Fire	442	692	504	1638
	Chocolate Almond	2286	2399	1857	6542
	Chocolate Hazelnut	3330	3278.75	4937.5	11546.25
	Chocolate Pistachio	766.5	973	791	2530.5
	Extra Dark Chocolate	1059	1126.5	1627.5	3813
	Milk Chocolate	6100	6135	6252	18487
	Orange Chocolate	1390.5	1275	1179	3844.5
	Peanut Butter Chocolate		103.75	110	213.75
	White Chocolate	623	678	1104	2405

With only a few clicks the entire table is transformed into a pro level report, check below.

Customer	Product	2011	2012	2013	Grand Total
Agnes Whole Foods		$ 1,008	$ 1,386	$ 1,484	$ 3,878
	Bacon Chocolate	$ 34	$ 36	$ 38	$ 108
	Chilli Chocolate Fire	$ 118	$ 250	$ 138	$ 506
	Chocolate Almond	$ 23	$ 154	$ 218	$ 395
	Chocolate Hazelnut	$ 455	$ 258	$ 480	$ 1,193
	Chocolate Pistachio	$ -	$ 130	$ -	$ 130
	Extra Dark Chocolate	$ 221	$ 339	$ 281	$ 840
	Milk Chocolate	$ 88	$ 20	$ 218	$ 326
	Orange Chocolate	$ 38	$ -	$ 66	$ 104
	White Chocolate	$ 32	$ 200	$ 45	$ 277
Crazy Oats		$ 16,330	$ 16,709	$ 18,653	$ 51,692
	Bacon Chocolate	$ 288	$ 20	$ 266	$ 574
	Banana Chocolate	$ 45	$ 28	$ 25	$ 98
	Chilli Chocolate Fire	$ 442	$ 692	$ 504	$ 1,638
	Chocolate Almond	$ 2,286	$ 2,399	$ 1,857	$ 6,542
	Chocolate Hazelnut	$ 3,330	$ 3,279	$ 4,938	$ 11,546
	Chocolate Pistachio	$ 767	$ 973	$ 791	$ 2,531
	Extra Dark Chocolate	$ 1,059	$ 1,127	$ 1,628	$ 3,813
	Milk Chocolate	$ 6,100	$ 6,135	$ 6,252	$ 18,487
	Orange Chocolate	$ 1,391	$ 1,275	$ 1,179	$ 3,845
	Peanut Butter Chocolate	$ -	$ 104	$ 110	$ 214
	White Chocolate	$ 623	$ 678	$ 1,104	$ 2,405

Pivot Tables are Perfect Prototyping Tools

At times you might get confused about what to do with the data that you have been presented with, you might get confused on how to organize it in the excel worksheet for better analysis. By using the pivot table, you will have a chance to test the data and see the results. If you are not satisfied with the results, then you can adjust accordingly, but if the results are perfect, you can proceed.

Experiment with different layouts until you find the one that best suits you. For instance, let's say that you need to tell the IT the kind of a report that the management needs to analyze sales for a given year, the IT team need to code that report in the web app that they manage. By the use of pivot table, you can start off by adding the products and sales to the pivot table.

Product	Total
Bacon Chocolate	$ 3,754
Banana Chocolate	$ 729
Chilli Chocolate Fire	$ 18,654
Chocolate Almond	$ 33,146
Chocolate Hazelnut	$ 77,594
Chocolate Pistachio	$ 6,871
Extra Dark Chocolate	$ 35,637
Milk Chocolate	$ 68,244
Orange Chocolate	$ 16,133
Peanut Butter Chocolate	$ 3,510
White Chocolate	$ 14,199
Grand Total	$ 278,470

Then you need to key in details such as the date.

Product	2011				2012		
	Qtr1	Qtr2	Qtr3	Qtr4	Qtr1	Qtr2	Qtr3
Bacon Chocolate	$ -	$ 134	$ 300	$ -	$ -	$ 1,182	$ 378
Banana Chocolate	$ -	$ 46	$ 125	$ -	$ -	$ 195	$ 94
Chilli Chocolate Fire	$ 1,528	$ 534	$ 1,752	$ 1,206	$ 930	$ 1,438	$ 1,408
Chocolate Almond	$ 5,207	$ 419	$ 118	$ 3,370	$ 5,226	$ 815	$ 149
Chocolate Hazelnut	$ 5,534	$ 3,285	$ 4,091	$ 8,490	$ 4,684	$ 4,913	$ 4,265
Chocolate Pistachio	$ 782	$ 193	$ 145	$ 908	$ 1,124	$ 277	$ 242
Extra Dark Chocolate	$ 7,082	$ 1,269	$ 1,149	$ 896	$ 6,264	$ 3,404	$ 792
Milk Chocolate	$ 7,409	$ 2,438	$ 4,890	$ 8,877	$ 7,213	$ 2,196	$ 4,532
Orange Chocolate	$ -	$ 3,765	$ 1,115	$ -	$ -	$ 3,596	$ 1,758
Peanut Butter Chocolate	$ 86	$ 26	$ -	$ 583	$ 261	$ 43	$ 105
White Chocolate	$ 2,630	$ 631	$ 999	$ 386	$ 2,093	$ 646	$ 959
Grand Total	$ 30,258	$ 12,740	$ 14,684	$ 24,715	$ 27,795	$ 18,703	$ 14,682

Okay, this report is not, but it's too broad, let's try and see how quarters would work in rows

Product	Date	2011	2012	2013	Grand Total
Bacon Chocolate		$ 434	$ 1,560	$ 1,760	$ 3,754
	Qtr2	$ 134	$ 1,182	$ 1,252	$ 2,568
	Qtr3	$ 300	$ 378	$ 508	$ 1,186
Banana Chocolate		$ 171	$ 289	$ 269	$ 729
	Qtr2	$ 46	$ 195	$ 169	$ 410
	Qtr3	$ 125	$ 94	$ 100	$ 319
Chilli Chocolate Fire		$ 5,020	$ 6,224	$ 7,410	$ 18,654
	Qtr1	$ 1,528	$ 930	$ 1,292	$ 3,750
	Qtr2	$ 534	$ 1,438	$ 1,322	$ 3,294
	Qtr3	$ 1,752	$ 1,408	$ 1,892	$ 5,052
	Qtr4	$ 1,206	$ 2,448	$ 2,904	$ 6,558
Chocolate Almond		$ 9,114	$ 12,321	$ 11,711	$ 33,146
	Qtr1	$ 5,207	$ 5,226	$ 3,858	$ 14,291
	Qtr2	$ 419	$ 815	$ 705	$ 1,939
	Qtr3	$ 118	$ 149	$ 194	$ 461
	Qtr4	$ 3,370	$ 6,131	$ 6,954	$ 16,455
Chocolate Hazelnut		$ 21,400	$ 22,655	$ 33,539	$ 77,594
	Qtr1	$ 5,534	$ 4,684	$ 5,974	$ 16,191
	Qtr2	$ 3,285	$ 4,913	$ 4,268	$ 12,465
	Qtr3	$ 4,091	$ 4,265	$ 5,481	$ 13,838
	Qtr4	$ 8,490	$ 8,794	$ 17,816	$ 35,100
Chocolate Pistachio		$ 2,028	$ 2,893	$ 1,950	$ 6,871
	Qtr1	$ 782	$ 1,124	$ 592	$ 2,497

Now this works, you have something that you can call a report that you can now send to the IT team. This report will enable them to have the exact idea of what you want to be created.

You have now witnessed how pivot table an excellent prototyping tool. Besides they play a more significant role in helping you understand the kind of data you need to collect, how you can analyze it and send it to the relevant parties without delays.

Pivot Tables can Examine Any Type of Data

Most of the examples of pivot tables offered on the web concentrate on the sales data. Someone might think that the pivot table is only used in sales data, but that's not the case. A pivot table can be used to analyze any data that you want. For instance, let's assume that you have the employee list and you are required to create a simple breakdown per each department. Let's check the following data.

ID	First	Last	Department
00610	Mick	Lam	Fufillment
00798	Curtis	Zimmerman	Sales
00841	Thomas	Ford	Fufillment
00886	Dorothy	Cogar	Fufillment
00622	Traci	Brown	Marketting
00601	Mary	Hannan	Engineering
00869	Esther	Kittinger	Marketting
00867	Linda	Thomas	Fufillment
00785	Bernice	Wilson	Fufillment
00648	Sarah	Burton	Support
00604	Kevin	Grizzle	Sales
00352	Chad	Jackson	Engineering
00623	Jerry	Brooks	Sales
00428	Alene	Helsel	Marketting
00491	Jennifer	Simpson	Sales
00625	Jordan	Barrera	Engineering
00184	John	Priolo	Sales
00893	Jason	Ward	Sales
00645	Edward	Taylor	Fufillment
00120	Teresa	Wilson	Fufillment
00331	Debbie	Jackson	Support

By looking at this set of data, you can push it to the pivot table to generate a report, and within a minute, this is what you will get:

Department	Count	%
Engineering	61	20%
Fufillment	69	23%
Marketting	55	18%
Sales	69	23%
Support	46	15%
Grand Total	300	100%

Now you can follow the pattern and see how easy it is; you have to start with the raw data that you have collected. Then you need to push this data to the pivot table within a fraction of a minute; you will have your report.

Finally, You can Quickly Update Pivot Tables

In this dynamic world, data is always changing and the experience that you had yesterday might not be the same with what you will encounter tomorrow. Pivot tables are different from the other tools found in excel; they don't update automatically. The beginners always get confused because they change the source data expecting that even the pivot table will adjust accordingly but that does not happen.

To update the pivot table, you need first to refresh the source data. Once you get started with pivot tables, you must have realized by now that data refreshing is the best feature of pivot tables because this is the moment when Excel does the rest of work for you automatically. To update your report, the first step you need to carry is paste over the data you had collected previously. Because the information is contained in the excel table, the table will range automatically and adjust to include even the data that you have to add.

Chapter Exercise

1. Apart from the above-listed benefits, what other benefits do you think the pivot table offers especially in business?

2. How is a pivot table able to work correctly without the use of formulas?

3. How does a pivot table assist you to eliminate errors on the on your reports?

4. How do you refresh the source data on excel spreadsheets?

5. Upon updating a Pivot Table, it always loses the formatting like the column width. How can this be corrected?

Chapter Seven: Types of PivotTables

If you have been keenly following the pivot tables in different websites, you might realize by now that majority of those websites use sales data as their examples. It doesn't mean that pivot tables cannot be created for other data; they can be. The reason why sales data is widely used as examples is that sale deals with money, and it is quite easy to use sales because all companies at least have sales data at any given point. If this got you confused, you should know that pivot tables could be used to handle any data. Any time you want to work with data, pivot tables should always be in your mind.

To explain how essential and powerful pivot tables are, below are five exciting examples of pivot tables that you might not have seen before. Each type will be followed by a detailed elaboration so that you can understand what each type entails and how you can use it.

Time Tracking Pivot Table

Strategic planning is everything for the business. If you need to log in different times for different clients or projects, this task will not be as stressful. Pivot table summarizes all the data that you push to it to feature your desired format. Let's say that you want to see the information on a weekly basis; excel provides a function known as WEEKNUM function. You also have the chance to see the layout of the traditional timetable.

Imagine being in a situation whereby you are dealing with different clients; you need different time to log into each one of them to report the progress of your projects. You need reporting time for different clients. Of course, there are a lot of applications dedicated to time tracking, but the pivot table is the best of all. All that you need to record is the date, time spent in doing that particular project, the name of the client and finally the project. After you have keyed in all the relevant details consistently, you should end up having something like this:

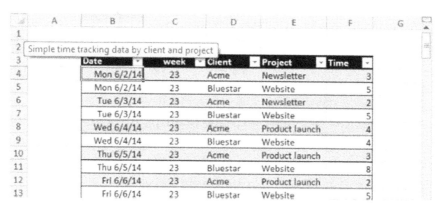

You must have noticed that there are no blank spaces between the data cells; you need to enhance consistency when you are entering the data to avoid the problems that might arise when pushing the data to the pivot table. You might want to view your time by weeks or days. Your pivot table will appear as follows:

Sum of Time		week								
Client	Project	23	24	25	26	27	28	29	30	Total
Acme	Newsletter	5	-	-	-	5	-	-	-	10
	Product launch	9	-	-	-	9	-	-	-	18
	Website	-	2	2	2	-	2	2	2	12
Bluestar	Website	27	18	18	18	27	18	18	18	162
Simple cube	Explainer video	-	13	21	21	-	21	21	21	118
	Banner ad	-	9	-	-	-	-	-	-	9
Total		41	42	41	41	41	41	41	41	329

			Date					
Sum of Time								
Client	Project		Mon 6/23	Tue 6/24	Wed 6/25	Thu 6/26	Fri 6/27	Total
Acme	Website		1	-	-	-	1	2
Bluestar	Website		5	2	1	5	5	18
Simple cub	Explainer video		3	5	8	3	2	21
Total			9	7	9	8	8	41

A critical point to note is that, once you filter a different week number, the pivot table develops a new sheet that shows the days of the week.

It is also important to note that, when you add a name column to the data, you have the chance to track and report time for multiple clients. Besides, you could also include a rate column to the same data the use of the pivot table to create a summary of the billing rate of the time logged.

User Activity in a Web Portal Pivot Table

Imagine of a situation whereby, you are presented with data dump from a company's website, the website provides product information to various partners. The partners of this website login consistently throughout the year. You decide to open up the data to take a look, and you find that there are over 30000 registered users; the data might appear as follows;

	A	B	C	D	E	F	G
1	First_Name	Last_Name	Email	User_Status	Cour	User_Creation	Last_Login
2	Patrick	Agcaoili	patrick@evideo.net	Inactive	0	Tue 4/16/13	Tue 4/16,
3	Josh	Aadar	josh@telerexpartners.biz	Inactive	5	Mon 5/31/10	Sat 4/27,
4	Veronica	Aamir	veronica@telerexpartners.biz	Inactive	2	Mon 10/3/11	Wed 12/21,
5	Michael	Aamir	michael@businessinc.net	Inactive	4	Tue 11/6/12	Fri 11/9,
6	Daniel	Aananou	daniel@dimensiontech.net	Active	5	Thu 4/21/11	Mon 2/10,
7	Liron	Aarons	liron@datelgroup.net	Active	0	Wed 11/6/13	Mon 11/11,
8	Johan	Aarons	johan@missionvoice.net	Inactive	0	Thu 3/10/11	Thu 3/10,
9	Gary	Aaronson	gary@interwire.com	Active	4	Fri 5/24/13	Mon 11/25,
10	Scott	Aas	scott@cytekbrothers.biz	Inactive	0	Wed 11/9/11	Mon 9/24,
11	Roberto	Aastad	roberto@execulinknet.com	Active	3	Thu 10/6/11	Fri 1/24,
12	Karmozyn	Abablo	karmozyn@spccomplete.com	Inactive	2	Tue 6/5/12	Wed 6/6,
13	Denise	Abad	denise@hbconglomerate.me	Active	0	Wed 11/6/13	Tue 1/7,

This table shows just a sample of the data that you may find when you log in. Let 's say that the boss wants to get some necessary information from you like the number of users that are active currently, the number of users joining every month or what partner has the highest number of user accounts among others. So is it possible to deliver this kind of information within one hours' time?

Before panicking and decide whether you will delegate the work or do it confidently, you should know that that this kind of data can be analyzed entirely in pivot tables, it will only take a short while, and you will have sufficient time to do some other things. This is what pivot tables will have for you:

User_Status	Total
Active	16,829
Inactive	16,240
Suspended	30
Grand Total	33,099

A simple summary of all users by status

It's impressive to note that there are even a section of suspended members though you did not ask for that. Who knew there could be suspended users? It's only the pivot tables. Then go for the top ten partners by the number of users that are currently active. The high ten-value filter quickly does it; this is what you should expect:

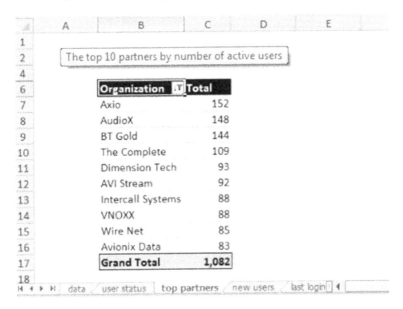

Class List Pivot Table

Let us look for an example whereby you want to coordinate sign-ups for a class offered on Mondays, Wednesdays, and Fridays. Every day when there are sign-ups, you expect to have something that looks like this:

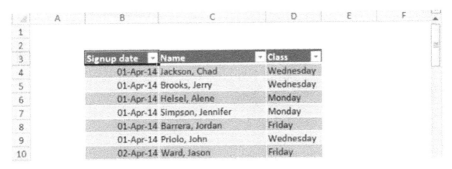

Your primary responsibility here is to send a report to the instructor at the begging of each day to sow the number of current registrations. The data is quite small in this case, if you have to generate the report manually, you need to employ some filtering and sorting techniques, and the devastating thing is that you will need to repeat this process daily, however, it is automatic when you are using the pivot tables. It's quite simple when you employ the pivot tables, create a simple pivot table that summarizes the class day, you should have something similar to this

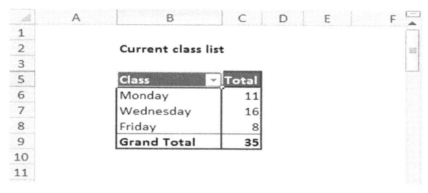

When you add the name, you can come up with a full class list that looks something like this:

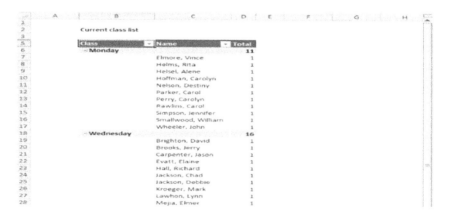

Instrument Measurement Pivot Table

Let's assume that you have measurement data from instruments that records, relative humidity, temperature, rainfall, dew point. You might have a data that looks something like this.

	A	B	C	D	E	F	G
1							
2		Instrument readings (every 2 minutes)					
3							
4		Date	Time	Temp, °C	RH, %	DewPt, °C	
5		8/21/2014	3:00:00 PM	19.79	58.24	11.37	
6		8/21/2014	3:02:00 PM	19.98	60.04	12.01	
7		8/21/2014	3:04:00 PM	20.34	60.93	12.57	
8		8/21/2014	3:06:00 PM	20.63	60.74	12.80	
9		8/21/2014	3:08:00 PM	20.89	60.45	12.97	
10		8/21/2014	3:10:00 PM	20.98	60.80	13.15	
11		8/21/2014	3:12:00 PM	20.72	59.56	12.59	
12		8/21/2014	3:14:00 PM	20.79	60.20	12.82	
13		8/21/2014	3:16:00 PM	20.46	59.55	12.34	
14		8/21/2014	3:18:00 PM	20.58	60.05	12.58	
15		8/21/2014	3:20:00 PM	20.84	58.49	12.42	
16		8/21/2014	3:22:00 PM	20.87	58.50	12.44	
17		8/21/2014	3:24:00 PM	20.37	59.53	12.24	
18		8/21/2014	3:26:00 PM	20.41	59.93	12.39	
19		8/21/2014	3:28:00 PM	20.44	59.19	12.22	
20		8/21/2014	3:30:00 PM	20.56	59.59	12.44	

You need to quick breakdown to show the average reading of these instruments per hour. You can do this activity manually by constructing your formulas, but there is no need as you are going to waste a lot of your precious time. By pushing this data into the pivot table, you can efficiently add each of the above measurements as a value, and then you have to change the display from the sum to average. The result of this process will be a tidy summary which will display the average reading of each measurement per hour; check the example below. The average reading per hour will look like this in less than five minutes

Date	Time	Avg Temp, °C	Avg RH, %	Avg DewPt, °C
8/21/2014	3 PM	20.4	59.6	12.3
8/21/2014	4 PM	19.1	60.9	11.4
8/21/2014	5 PM	18.0	63.1	10.9
8/21/2014	6 PM	18.0	71.3	12.8
8/21/2014	7 PM	16.7	77.8	12.9
8/21/2014	8 PM	16.1	78.4	12.4
8/21/2014	9 PM	16.0	77.7	12.2
8/21/2014	10 PM	16.1	77.9	12.3
8/21/2014	11 PM	15.9	77.5	12.0
8/22/2014	12 AM	16.0	78.2	12.2
8/22/2014	1 AM	16.3	78.7	12.6
8/22/2014	2 AM	16.8	79.5	13.2
8/22/2014	3 AM	16.3	78.7	12.6
8/22/2014	4 AM	15.4	78.0	11.6
8/22/2014	5 AM	15.1	78.0	11.3

Average readings (by hour)

Email Sign Ups Pivot Tables

Email sign-ups are one of the underutilized options of pivot table thought it is imperative and exciting because of how you could easily solve problems. In case you are seeking to analyze the email sign-ups by dates to identify the days of the week that could be more successful, then the pivot table is your tool. The only thing that matters the most is having the data that you can add to the pivot table then excel will automatically do the rest of the work for you. If you want to narrow your data to feature special categories, pivot table allows you to do precisely that, besides you can have the chance to color-code your email signups.

In this case, let's assume that you are working with a client that is tracking the traffic of email sign-ups on their websites. The client is planning on embarking on, and a new promotion campaign and he wants you to investigate the best day for sign-ups in a week, by the data that they have collected. It can be somehow trick to include the day of the week because it is not found in the data. However, you can still add it by the use of weekday function. Your data looks something similar to this:

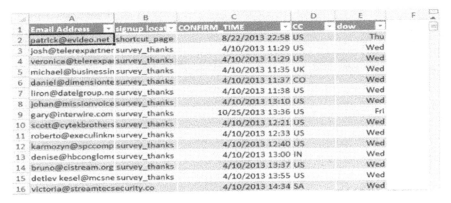

	A	B	C	D	E	F
1	Email Address	signup locat	CONFIRM TIME	CC	dow	
2	patrick@evideo.net	shortcut_page	8/22/2013 22:58	US	Thu	
3	josh@telerexpartner	survey_thanks	4/10/2013 11:29	US	Wed	
4	veronica@telerexpai	survey_thanks	4/10/2013 11:29	US	Wed	
5	michael@businessin	survey_thanks	4/10/2013 11:35	UK	Wed	
6	daniel@dimensionte	survey_thanks	4/10/2013 11:37	CO	Wed	
7	liron@datelgroup.ne	survey_thanks	4/10/2013 11:38	US	Wed	
8	johan@missionvoice	survey_thanks	4/10/2013 13:10	US	Wed	
9	gary@interwire.com	survey_thanks	10/25/2013 13:36	US	Fri	
10	scott@cytekbrothers	survey_thanks	4/10/2013 12:21	US	Wed	
11	roberto@execulinkn	survey_thanks	4/10/2013 12:33	US	Wed	
12	karmozyn@spccomp	survey_thanks	4/10/2013 12:40	US	Wed	
13	denise@hbconglome	survey_thanks	4/10/2013 13:00	IN	Wed	
14	bruno@cistream.org	survey_thanks	4/10/2013 13:37	US	Wed	
15	detlev kesel@mcsne	survey_thanks	4/10/2013 13:55	US	Wed	
16	victoria@streamtecsecurity.co		4/10/2013 14:34	SA	Wed	

Then an initial summary will look like this:

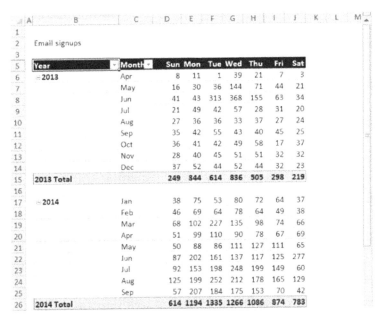

Email signups

Year	Month	Sun	Mon	Tue	Wed	Thu	Fri	Sat
2013	Apr	8	11	1	39	21	7	3
	May	16	30	36	144	71	44	21
	Jun	41	43	313	368	155	63	34
	Jul	21	49	42	57	28	31	20
	Aug	27	36	36	33	37	27	24
	Sep	35	42	55	43	40	45	25
	Oct	36	41	42	49	58	17	37
	Nov	28	40	45	51	51	32	32
	Dec	37	52	44	52	44	32	23
2013 Total		249	344	614	836	505	298	219
2014	Jan	38	75	53	80	72	64	37
	Feb	46	69	64	78	64	49	38
	Mar	68	102	227	135	98	74	66
	Apr	51	99	110	90	78	67	69
	May	50	88	86	111	127	111	65
	Jun	87	202	161	137	117	125	277
	Jul	92	153	198	248	199	149	60
	Aug	125	199	252	212	178	165	129
	Sep	57	207	184	175	153	70	42
2014 Total		614	1194	1335	1266	1086	874	783

By looking at the data, you realize that it is essential to display the total sign-ups in terms of percentages instead of using the number counts. When you set the email count to display the row percentage, the pivot table will automatically show a breakdown by the weekdays, besides you can add conditional formatting features to make the lower and the higher percentage distinctive. For instance, in this case, the green color depicts the higher percentages while the blue color represents, the lower percentage.

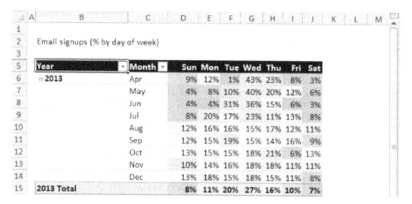

Email signups (% by day of week)

Year	Month	Sun	Mon	Tue	Wed	Thu	Fri	Sat
⊟2013	Apr	9%	12%	1%	43%	23%	8%	3%
	May	4%	8%	10%	40%	20%	12%	6%
	Jun	4%	4%	31%	36%	15%	6%	3%
	Jul	8%	20%	17%	23%	11%	13%	8%
	Aug	12%	16%	16%	15%	17%	12%	11%
	Sep	12%	15%	19%	15%	14%	16%	9%
	Oct	13%	15%	15%	18%	21%	6%	13%
	Nov	10%	14%	16%	18%	18%	11%	11%
	Dec	13%	18%	15%	18%	15%	11%	8%
2013 Total		8%	11%	20%	27%	16%	10%	7%

For more details, follow this link https://exceljet.net/blog/5-pivot-tables-you-probably-havent-seen-before

Monthly Reports

By using excel provided 'Group" feature, you can quickly summarize days, weeks, moths information into weekly, monthly or annual reports. However, you can even group information by month only to see the trend of sales over the past few months, or you can as well group them by month and year, hence have an opportunity to see the performance of each month. Using the pivot table can help you summarize a significant amount of data into a simple single spreadsheet.

Chapter Exercise

1. Identify various pivot tables that you can use and how you can work on each of them to achieve your goals.

2. Because you have already gone through the various types of pivot tables that you can create, can you recall how you can use a pivot table to remember how you can track your time to ensure you serve all your clients satisfactory?

3. Identify one or several areas that you think that they are slow in operation, but the same process undertaken can be done correctly by pivot table to enhance efficiency.

4. Can you illustrate how pivot tables can apply to small and medium businesses?

Chapter Eight: Advantages of Working with Pivot Tables

The main advantage of working with pivot tables is that they allow you to see how the data work behaves when you introduce some changes. A pivot table is one of the available excel tool so far that enable the users to have total insight into data analytics. Besides users can generate multiple reports from this tool from the same data within a single file within seconds

Pivot tables can work correctly with SQL exports. SQL is an abbreviation for *the structured query language*. Its primary role is to request information from the database. Over the decades, SQL has been the leading query language for database management system running on PCs and mainframes. If the pivot table tool is used on the Microsoft Excel, then the tool integrates well with SQL export.

Besides, the data held in the pivot tables are easier to segment. By using the pivot tables, users can segment the analytics gathered into the database.

Pivot table enables you to create instant data whether you directly program equations to the pivot table or whether you rely on the excel formula. It doesn't take you a lot of time to add all the data together to create a report. Besides generating a report manually has a couple of disadvantages because there might be an error in the formula, it consumes a lot of time. In case you need a different version of the report you have to go to the starting point again. However, the pivot table eliminates all these drawbacks because it is efficient, super-fast and reliable.

Chapter Exercise

1. Identify other advantages that one can get from using the pivot tables?

2. What are some of the problems you are likely to encounter while creating pivot tables if you didn't follow the steps precisely?

Chapter Nine: Application Support of Pivot Table

The functionality of a pivot table is a result of several basic spreadsheet applications and database software; it is also found in some other data visualization tools and business packages.

Initially, Google documents had allowed for the creation of the pivot table gadget that was referred to as panorama analytics. However, by the year 2011, this device proved to be problematic because limited functionality and slow processing speed in case of large data set.

Database Support for Pivot Tables

The SQL, an object that relates to the database management system, allows the pivot tables to be created using the *tablefunc* module. Also, the SQL fork enables pivot tables that use CONNECT storage engine to be functional.

Some of the popular databases that do not support pivot functionality directly, such as the Microsoft SQL server as well as SQLite can derail the functionality of the pivot table by using some embedded functions such as the dynamic SQL and subqueries. The challenge that faces pivoting in these kinds of scenarios are that the number of the output column must be well known at the time by which the query begins to execute. Pivoting, in this case, will not be possible because the number of columns relies on the data itself. This means that, for pivoting to work, the names must be coded hard or the query must have been created dynamically for it to execute by the data.

When it comes to online analytical processing, excel pivot tables contains a feature that directly queries an OLAP server for data retrieval instead of relying on the excel spreadsheet to obtain the data. In this setup, the pivot table acts as a simple client of an OLAP server. The pivot table not only allows the connection to Microsoft analysis service.

Conclusion

We hope that this tutorial will serve you a great deal in handling your data more efficiently. Again, if you didn't know why you would require the input of a pivot table, now you know how much it can save your time and also help you produce quality reports. However, a crucial point to note is that you should follow the steps of building the pivot table very carefully to avoid the error notifications. We also hope that the skills you have learned in this tutorial will help you to plan on how to deal with different dynamics of your data for decision-making. This is a powerful tool that can help your business or project to have a competitive edge in the market by enhancing quality and efficiency. We are optimistic that we have been able to address all your questions regarding the pivot tables.

www.ingramcontent.com/pod-product-compliance
Lightning Source LLC
Chambersburg PA
CBHW031240050326
40690CB00007B/896